D1478028

A
History Lover's
Guide
to Mississippi

A
HISTORY LOVER'S
GUIDE
TO
MISSISSIPPI

by Mary Ann Wells

QRP BOOKS
Brandon, Mississippi

DEDICATION

To Benjamin

Manufactured in the United States of America
Designed by Barney McKee
Library of Congress Catalog Card Number: 87-92248

Library of Congress Cataloging-in-Publication Data

Wells, Mary Ann, 1944-
    A history lover's guide to Mississippi.

    Includes index.
    1. Mississippi--Description and travel--
1981-   --Guide-books.   2. Historic sites--
Mississippi--Guide-books.   3. Mississippi--History,
Local.   I. Title.
F339.3.W45   1988   917.62'0463   87-92248
ISBN 0-937552-22-4

Table of Contents

Introduction

Mississippi is a history lover's dream. Sultry southern breezes scented with magnolias can easily stir yearnings even among the most practical people for a closer look at the mythical romantic lifestyles that have brought the state notoriety. History lovers will find their daydreams of other times moving closer to reality in a state where entire towns (Natchez, Port Gibson, Holly Springs, Carrollton, etc.) have their architecture, manners and mores so firmly planted in past eras.

Civil War buffs can still hear the roar of the cannons, the haunting memory of battle's turmoil, at living history displays and monuments such as the National Military Park and Cemetery at Vicksburg. In the park the warring armies' past activities are augmented with a Union gunboat rescued from the mud of the Yazoo River 100 years after the conflict and now on display as a museum.

But the history is deeper, richer and more complex than the terrible civil conflict. Natchez, the seat of government for the Great Sun, ruler of the Natchez Indians before permanent white settlements, is today the site of the excavated Grand Village of the Great Sun. A museum on the site as well as replicas of villagers' farmsteads offer a very different view of Mississippi. Often modern Mississippi Choctaw Indians come to the village to dance or to entertain visitors with Indian stickball games as well as to demonstrate native crafts.

Mississippi is the ancestral homeland of the Choctaw and Chickasaw Indians. Nanih Waiya, the mother mound, which according to myth, gave birth to the founders of both tribes, is now a park in central Mississippi.

Other sites of mythical proportions, such as Fort Adams, have become ghost towns. In one of the most poignant stories in American literature, *The Man Without a Country,* a fictional Philip Nolan was imprisoned at Fort Adams. The fort was a non-fictional outpost on the far southwestern border of the

USA at the beginning of the 19th century, and a real-life Philip
Nolan, a romantic Irishman and bold frontiersman, was a
confidant of the fort's commander.

Paths and trails, as well as the Mississippi River, took
travelers north from Fort Adams to the Natchez Trace and the
main overland highway through the old southwest. Today, the
Natchez Trace Parkway cuts diagonally through the state and
straight through the heart of early American history. Native
American merchants, Spanish fortune hunters, French explorers, British traders, American militiamen and a host of
others traveled the Trace. Andrew Jackson was once a frequent
traveler on the road. He married Rachel Robards in the vicinity
of the Trace, north of Washington, Mississippi, and traveled
northward to Tennessee with her on a trip shortly afterwards.

The natural beauty of the Trace might inspire idyllic journeys
in modern times, but the rigors of the frontier probably
dimmed its charm for all but the most dedicated naturalists in
the early 19th century when John James Audubon wandered
along its southern-most stretches. The artist/naturalist painted
the birds on the southern end of the Trace while he sojourned
in the area.

Famous men, as well as the controversial, flocked to early
Mississippi. Aaron Burr was arraigned on charges of treason on
the grounds of Jefferson College at Washington, Adams
County. Perhaps the most famous and controversial Mississippian of all, Jefferson Davis, a dashing frontier soldier whose first
wife was the daughter of US President Zachary Taylor, became
a general in the Mexican War, a representative, then senator in
the US Congress, President Franklin Pierce's Secretary of War
and finally President of the Confederate States of America.
Davis grew up near Woodville, a place still considered to have
much of the look of a 19th century southern town.

Further south, Davis' final home faces the Gulf across a 26-
mile-long strand of white sand beach at Biloxi. For modest fees
excursion boats carry visitors 12-miles out from Biloxi and
Gulfport to Ship Island, one of the Barrier Islands. Its beaches
were the landing site for some of Mississippi's first European
colonists. The island's deep-water harbor was the staging point

for the British armada that came to attack New Orleans in the War of 1812. The site of Federal military prisons for Union soldier-convicts as well as captured Confederates POWs, the island has now reverted to a tropic-like beach paradise.

The history of the coast has a heavy French accent in contrast with the predominant Scotch-Irish-British tone found in the rest of the state's heritage. But Mississippi's cultural traditions are never one dimensional. Often they are spiced with subtle African and Native American influences that add a zest seldom found elsewhere.

The places that nurtured music, religion, art, literature, industry and agriculture across the ages—from pre-Columbian days through the present—will delight visitors who come seeking understanding of the state's past. This book is a sampler of those places.

Places included in this guide are sites where significant historical incidents occurred or places that by their nature reflect a true picture of some facet of the past. Visits to these places offer a feeling of spiritual fulfillment to those seeking a link with the past.

Sites were chosen in some instances because they represent geographic regions and are near other sites, as well as being places of historic interest in their own right. By including sites from all geographic regions of the state as well as from a broad spectrum of historic endeavors/events, a clearer picture of Mississippi's past is attained.

All sites included are easily reached by family automobile throughout the year with the exception of Ship Island which is served by excursion boats during the Gulf Coast tourist season (usually measured from April through Labor Day).

Mississippi is a very relaxed and casual place. Visitors should not be surprised if various enterprises don't open or close on a precise schedule. Call or write to verify hours for any given day at special attractions.

One of the best sources of general information for travelers in Mississippi is the Tourism Division of the state Department of Economic Development. Address: P.O. Box 22825, Jackson, MS 39205. Telephone (toll free) 800-647-2290.

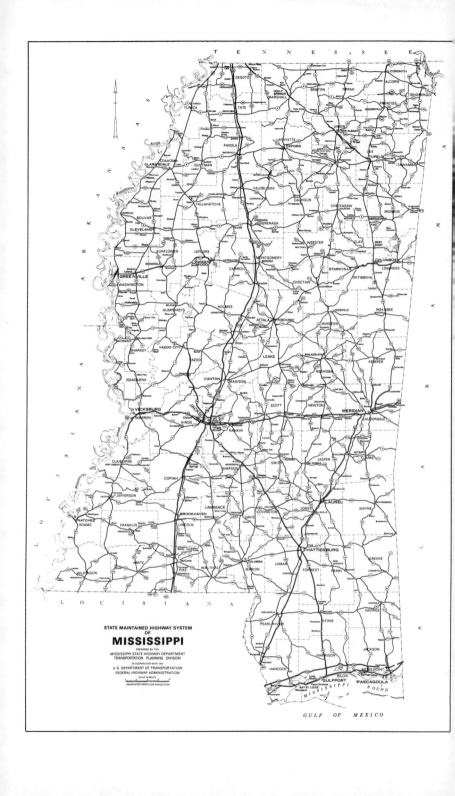

STATE MAINTAINED HIGHWAY SYSTEM
OF
MISSISSIPPI

PREPARED BY THE
MISSISSIPPI STATE HIGHWAY DEPARTMENT
TRANSPORTATION PLANNING DIVISION

IN COOPERATION WITH THE
U.S. DEPARTMENT OF TRANSPORTATION
FEDERAL HIGHWAY ADMINISTRATION

SCALE IN MILES

TRANSVERSE MERCATOR PROJECTION

1

Fort Adams, Pond, and Pinckneyville

Mississippi ghost towns keep their secrets well. The all-too willing vegetation, thick and rampant, slips over the remains of the past, covers and camouflages the places and things that men leave behind. Cloaked in a leafy mantle, the ghost town of Fort Adams passes itself off as a collection of fishing and hunting camps clustered around a few permanent residences, a country store and a church.

The high green hills on the back side of the town are loess bluffs, a rippled buffer carved from ancient sands blown into the area during the Ice Age. The Mississippi River, over two miles out across the flat fields behind the store, was less than a hundred yards from the main street back before the turn of the century.

Locals in the store point out the highest bluff where they say are the overgrown remains of an "old civil war fort." They claim gun placements were visible as late as the 1940s.

"Nothing up there now," the storekeeper says, "nothing but a monument to Philip Nolan." He quickly warns the area is off limits, private property, and that permission must be obtained from an out-of-town owner before anyone can go exploring.

"There's nothing to do once you get here except turn around and go back," the storekeeper says.

A historic marker on Mississippi Highway 24 west of Woodville announces the approach to the town and its most famous association.

Philip Nolan slept here, inside prison walls in a story by Edward Everett Hale entitled, *The Man Without A Country*. The line between truth and fiction has become so blurred, the fact that there was a real Philip Nolan and he wasn't the man in

Fort Adams' main street. Today the early settlement is virtually a ghost town.

the story is often lost. The real Philip Nolan was an adventurer, map maker, correspondent of Thomas Jefferson's, captor of wild horses, smuggler, possibly a spy, maybe a double agent, leader of an advance party for a shadowy invasion force into Texas, and confidant of the notorious General James Wilkinson who really was the commander of the fort here at the turn of the 18th century.

The real Philip Nolan was born in Ireland, lived in Natchez and died in a Texas shoot-out with Mexican militia forces. Actually his life seems a lot more interesting than that of Hale's *Man-Without-A-Country* who was tried for treason, in the process renounced the USA, and was sentenced to live out his life on ships at sea, never to set foot on land.

History books tell the story the secretive ghost town hides. In the late 1700s a fort named in honor of President John Adams was built on a hill the English had named Loftus Heights. Before that the hill was called *Roche a Davion* for a French priest who established a mission here among the Tunica Indians in the late 1600s. For the fledgling American republic, Fort Adams was a port of entry, an outpost on the far southwestern border of the new nation.

Indians gathered here in the early 1800s to negotiate the Treaty of Fort Adams between their Choctaw nation and the USA. For the Indians some of the most important issues addressed by the treaty were trading rules and regulations among the two nations, and passage of citizens through one nation to the other. The Civil War activity here was mainly a footnote to the earlier dramas—real and imaginary.

Fort Adams had a neighbor community a few miles away at the settlement of Pinckneyville, the camp site and starting point for the surveyors who accompanied Andrew Ellicott as he marked the 31st parallel between American and Spanish territory in the late 18th century. There's an unmarked road at the edge of town (on MS 24) that cuts across the loess bluffs to Pinckneyville via Pond.

The steep hills and ravines of the bluffs are wilderness terrain, 1200 acres of which have been set aside as the Clark Creek Natural Area. There's a 50-foot waterfall in the area and a unique perspective of wild Mississippi. Known as the Tunica Hills the area's treasures include Indian artifacts and exotic wildflowers and plants—some of which are just now being "discovered" by botanists.

Visitors are warned in a Mississippi Department of Wildlife Conservation bulletin that they "should be in good physical shape and conditioned to rigorous hiking" if they plan to venture more than a short distance into the area. But that's just the beginning. The bulletin also advises bringing a compass, a map and water. First-time visitors are further cautioned to go with someone who knows the area. There's no overnight camping.

The parking area for Clark Creek is about 300 yards from the Pond General Store at Pond, Mississippi, another village that has dissolved into the mists of time except for the store which is still in operation. Open seven days a week, the store with its dazzling brass turn-of-the-century cash register, now serves as a community quick-stop, mini-market. Dress-maker dummies, plows, kerosene lamps and those mysterious items that were the working tools of the storekeeper in the 1880s make the store an unself-conscious museum.

According to Norman Chaffin, owner of the Pond Store, the place name comes from the pond the county built as a watering place for the oxen, horses and mules which were used in hauling cotton and other produce five or six miles across the bluffs to Fort Adams for trans-shipment on the river. The pond is still intact, across the road from the store.

Chaffin also owns the small herd of donkeys that wander about Pond, sticking their heads in car windows and guilelessly conning visitors into a scratch behind the ears and maybe a sack of Cheetos. His wife Liz's father once owned the store and she is a willing storyteller of the establishment's earlier days. Her father worked for a transplanted Russian-Jewish storekeeper, Julius Lemkowitz, who spoke several languages and had been trained as both a lawyer and physician in Russia. He arrived at such a time that Liz speculates he must have been involved in some intrigue such as the Trotsky—Stalin split after the Bolshevik Revolution. Liz has a large collection of the gentleman's papers and possessions that support her speculations. She eagerly shares stories of the store's history as well as that of the nearby communities of Fort Adams and Pinckneyville.

Back on the road to Pinckneyville the thick, lush undergrowth laps out at the highway, little by little eating away at the blacktop. Somewhere out there, in the bushes, under the trees, in the tangle of vines and weeds is the campsite, and the ghostly remains of the frontier town that sprang up in the wake of the surveyors, somewhere before you cross the boundary into Louisiana. Liz Chaffin warns that the only marker you'll find commemorates the grave of Oliver Pollock, the man credited with inventing the dollar sign, being one of the chief financial backers of the American Revolution and bankrolling Thomas Jefferson's Lewis and Clark Expedition. According to local legends Merriwether Lewis and Pollock met and became friends when Lewis was stationed at Fort Adams in its early days. The same legends claim the highway passes through the old Pinckneyville Cemetery over the bones and dust of the dead. The moss-shrouded oaks massed along the road may shield the spirits and ghosts of the area's pioneers as well as the ghost of the town.

Fort Adams is located at the end of MS 24 West, about 20 miles from Woodville. Pond and Pinckneyville are located on the Pinckneyville Road which runs off MS 24 just west of Woodville. There is a sign for the Clark Creek Natural Area at the junction of the Pinckneyville Road and MS 24.

Some accommodations are available in Woodville. There are no facilities, accommodations or restaurants at Fort Adams, Pond or Pinckneyville. You can purchase gas and picnic supplies at Fort Adams or Pond. The Clark Creek Natural Area forms a perfect setting for a woodland picnic. Even the timid can enjoy venturing into the edge of the wilderness.

Liz Chaffin sometimes organizes tours of local plantation homes at Thanksgiving. For information write to her at the Pond Store, Rt. 2, Box 860, Woodville, MS 39669. Telephone 601-888-4426.

2
Woodville and Rosemont

On a lazy Sunday afternoon the bus station across the street from the Wilkinson County Courthouse is one of the few establishments open for business in Woodville. The bus station's worn red brick building, gripped in the lull, could have been lifted from an Edward Hopper painting. Summer splashes of crepe myrtle blossoms—from pale pink to deep lavender—wrap the town in a warm blanket of color. There is a sense of being suspended in time, of being isolated from the present, of being transposed into the past.

The past lingered here so long that once (prior to World War II) Harvard University's anthropology department proclaimed that Woodville best typified the Old South in appearance, customs and traditions. Enough of those traditions and appearances still prevail for Woodville to go on claiming that distinction.

The yellow brick courthouse, flanked by giant oaks, sits in the center of the town square and business district. One of the oaks on the courthouse's left side is a member of the American Society of Live Oaks, because of its size and age, and is called the Jefferson Davis Oak in honor of Woodville's favorite son.

The list of firsts for the town includes the first standard gauge railroad in America, the Old West Feliciana Railroad, which made its first run in 1842. The West Feliciana Railroad's home office with its massive columns and worn facade is the town's most impressive antebellum building despite intense competition from dozens of other stately structures. It is located on the southeast corner of the courthouse square, just down the street from the bus station.

The Methodist Episcopal Church South, the Baptist Church,

Antebellum street scene, modern day Woodville.

and St. Paul's Episcopal Church are all housed in buildings
more than 150 years old. During the Civil War the Episcopal
congregation sent their church bell to the Confederate General
P.G.T. Beauregard to be melted and recast as a cannon, with the
hope that ". . . the gentle tones . . . may be transmuted into
war's resounding rhyme to repel the ruthless invader from the
beautiful land of God . . ." The statement fairly well sums up
the local sentiment towards the war. The town claims to have
the state's "oldest business institution in continuous operation"
in its newspaper, *The Woodville Republican,* founded in 1823.
Andrew Marschalk, Mississippi's pioneer printer, is said to have
published a newspaper here as early as 1812.

Biographers of John James Aubudon say that when the
naturalist was living nearby at St. Francisville, Louisiana, he
came to Woodville to conduct dancing classes. Many wealthy
and educated people settled in the area giving the local cultural
activities variety and sophistication.

The town's architecture ranges from elegant "Southern Classic" to the simplified Mississippi planter's cottage, with

everything from Gothic, Victorian, and Federalist to Greek Revival in between. But the area's most famous antebellum home, Rosemont, is in the deep woods just outside of town. This is the modest planter's house Samuel Davis built in 1810 when he moved to Mississippi from Kentucky with his wife Jane, their youngest son, two-year-old Jefferson, and several older children.

Rosemont, a story-and-a-half house, featuring a front gable containing a Palladian window, was a compromise between the pragmatic southern planter's abode and the more refined Federal style of architecture. Today a rusty-red gravel road leads to the house from MS 24 East. The narrow unpaved road winds around the edge of a thick forest where light splatters through canopied trees like flecks of paint from an impressionistic painter's brush.

Visitors are treated to a short history lesson offering an interpretation of events more favorable to the President of the Confederacy than is normally heard. A graduate of the U.S.

Rosemont, Jefferson Davis' boyhood home, on the outskirts of Woodville.

Military Academy at West Point, a frontier soldier, a planter, veteran of the Mexican War, member of the U.S. House of Representatives, U.S. Senator, U.S. Secretary of War, Jefferson Davis' accomplishments seem phenomenal. Here he is remembered as an American patriot, a defender of the legacy of Thomas Jefferson, a believer in the constitution.

Gardens meander under oaks. Holly, wisteria and ivy grapple with marauding muscadine vines. Bird songs are heard above the constant static of the summer horde of locusts. The pine woods are encroaching on the boundaries set by split-rail fences. The house on its thin ridge has held tenaciously to its foothold in the wilderness for nearly two hundred years. At best it is a stand-off.

Inside the wide central hall separating the four rooms on the first floor, wall markings record the measurements of children over the years. A windowpane in the back bedroom bears the carvings of children's names, a cabinet contains a few mementoes of Sarah Knox Taylor, daughter of U.S. President Zachary Taylor and first wife of Jefferson Davis. The house sheltered five generations of the Davis family before being sold in 1895. Clarissa Fenner Pendelton, a relative of a close Davis family friend, bought the house to save the family the embarrassment of having it sold at sheriff's auction. In 1901 the Johnson family bought Rosemont, and it remained in that family until 1971 when it was purchased by Percival T. Beacroft, III.

Before 1971 the owners' meager resources saved the house from alterations. Until Beacroft bought the place, there was no electricity or indoor plumbing. With help from the Davis family, Beacroft has located and "brought home" many original Davis furnishings. On the wide back gallery, visitors are invited to sit and view the wilderness as they listen to a recording of an actress portraying Jane Davis tell how she and her husband Samuel decided to settle here. They named their new Mississippi home Poplar Grove. Later, due to her gardening skills, the place was renamed Rosemont. The back gallery looks out over a ravine where the spring house was once located. Down the steps, across the yard, the kitchen and outbuildings offer glimpses into the practicality of modest antebellum living.

Nearby on the "north knoll," a stoic iron fence stands guard around the family cemetery. Jane Davis and several of her children, grandchildren and other family members rest in the deep forest's peace. Every two years members of the Davis family still gather here for a reunion where Jane and Samuel's youngest son said, ". . . my memories begin."

Woodville is located at the junction of US 61 and MS 24 about 34 miles south of Natchez. Some accommodations are available in town. Restaurants are not always open. A walking tour of the town's historic district and other information about area attractions is available from the Woodville Civic Club, Inc., Box 814, Woodville, MS 39669. Telephone 601-888-6809.

Rosemont, located less than a mile from town on MS 24 East, is open from March through December 15, Monday through Friday, 10 a.m. to 4 p.m. Admission fee charged. Telephone 601-888-6809.

3

Kingston, Adams County and Church Hill, Jefferson County

The roads of rural Adams County slice through the loess hills, rolling over a landscape that was a farmer's dream of paradise in the late 1700's when settlers of British heritage came to the area.

Off of US Highway 61 less than five miles south of Natchez, the Kingston Road, designated by a historic marker, leads to the old Kingston town site. This was an enclave of loyalist British colonists transplanted from New Jersey in the late 1700s. The town is gone, but some of the settlers' planter-styled cottages survive, tucked in cedar groves or crested on hills, in the area known as the Jersey settlement. But the most poignant surviving material legacy of that early community is the churches, true architectural treasures that reflect the luster and longing of the antebellum soul.

The area is still populated by descendants of the original settlers who form an unbroken chain of family memberships in at least one of the churches. Kingston Methodist Church's members meet for worship services early Sunday mornings because it is on a charge with several other small congregations and must share a preacher. Oaks dripping Spanish moss shade outdoor tables waiting for the next dinner on the grounds. High brick steps on the far side of the church yard were erected in the early days as a dismounting stage for carriages and horses. Remnants of a brick paved yard peek through the sand and grass. Members say once the entire front yard of the church was paved with brick.

The stark white walls of the temple-like brick and stucco structure are relieved on the sides by high windows trimmed with green shutters. The front portico shelters birds' and

Kingston Methodist Church, Adams County.

hornets' nests on its ceiling's ledges. In true frontier spirit the
door is unlocked. Visitors step into a sanctuary of careful order,
an early American elegance of simple design, wooden pews and
brass chandeliers. The place seems to yearn for the strains of an
ancient hymn in the quiet of non-meeting hours.

Kingston Methodist Church with its slave gallery has been
called a "typical plantation church." Lorenzo Dow, the pioneer
evangelist and frontier preacher, sold his watch to purchase the
land for the church in 1803 according to local legends. The first
church was built of logs. A second church built of bricks,
erected in 1822, was destroyed by a tornado in 1840. The
present building was erected in 1856 and reflects the under-
stated elegance and affluence of plantation society at that time.

A historic marker about 12 miles down the Kingston Road
from US 61 stands sentinel across the road from the church. In
the field behind the sign, also across the road from the church,
is the grave of Caleb King, the founder of Kingston. A mile or
so further down the same road is the "Old Public Burying
Ground" of the Jersey settlers. The tombstones record the
names of early prominent settlers whose deaths date as far back
as 1784.

Back up the Kingston Road, just a few miles from US 61, is
Mount Carmel Road. It is at the intersection by Egypt Church,
a modern structure, and leads to Mount Carmel Church.
Looking like a trim but prosperous New England transplant to
the southern countryside, Mount Carmel has a Presbyterian
heritage but not an active congregation. The church sits on an
11-acre hillside and owns an adjoining 30 acres which supports
the building maintenance fund. Built in 1825 its white walls,
green shuttered windows, narrow porch with a slight starboard
list and domed cupola is a well-groomed ghostly reminder of
departed populations.

The people of Kingston didn't take their churches for granted
in early days. Shortly after their arrival here, while the American
Revolution occupied English attention, dominion of the
Natchez District was seized by Spain. The Spaniards instituted
their state religion as the only legal religion of the region. In
order to maintain their plantations and property, the Jersey

Mt. Carmel Presbyterian Church, Adams County.

settlers had to swear allegiance to the Spanish king and become Catholics—at least nominally.

Local storytellers have passed on legends of secret worship services, hidden Bibles, and fugitive Protestant preachers being captured and sent to New Orleans in chains. One documented case tells of Rev. Adam Cloud's bid for martyrdom in Adams County. For at least three years Rev. Cloud defied the Spaniards by conducting Protestant religious services and ceremonies. The record shows the Spaniards were remarkably tolerant of the lawbreaker, but finally lost patience with him and sent him down the river. Facing the Spanish magistrate in New Orleans, Rev. Cloud was given the choice of being sent to Spain for trial or of leaving Spanish territory and never returning. He took the latter option. With undiminished furor he later established a church just over the Adams County line in present day Jefferson County.

The English Gothic red brick Episcopal Christ Church today crowns Church Hill (on MS 553 just off the Natchez Trace

Christ Church, Church Hill, Jefferson County.

Parkway) where Rev. Cloud first erected a log church. The present building with its graceful ambience and tall hillside steps, erected in 1856, evokes such a romantic image, the television mini-series *North and South*'s producers shot scenes for their drama here.

To top off a Sunday service, youngsters run down the hillside steps and across the road to Wagner's Store. The weathered, time-worn building houses the Churchill U.S. Post Office in a caged corner, as well as the traditional staples of a country store. On a slow day store owner Adolph Wagner will join visitors on a bench out front for a Barq's or a Coke and pass on all the latest news as well as the most enduring local stories.

The stories, the oral history, and traditions of the area could be woven into the plots of endless southern dramas. The late Anna Farrar McCaleb, born in 1887 and living for almost a century, was one of the most engaging oral historians/story-tellers Kingston and the surrounding region ever produced. Her repertory started with her family arriving in their new home, lightly skipped over the American Revolution, continued into the rigors of the patriarchs traveling to New Orleans to swear allegiance to the Spanish crown and the Catholic church in order to retain their land, then veered into the light-hearted frivolous pre-Civil War world of her father and his contemporaries.

Her father, Thornton Farrar, went to medical school for a year before the Civil War, "Just to pass the time. He wasn't serious. A cousin went to Yale Law School. He was brilliant, but he wasn't serious either. They didn't have to be."

The Civil War devastated the family. Her father was charged with spying by the Union forces, taken prisoner of war, held at Ship Island for a while, then sent to Elmira, New York. But Mrs. McCaleb's most interesting saga was how after the war, due to the horrors of Reconstruction, Kingston families scrounged up the resources to send their young sons to France so they would not be "emotionally scarred." Her 24-year-old father was placed in charge of the youngsters. "They were supposed to be working on their education, but I think they mainly had a good time," she said.

Nearly all area family histories intertwine. The Sojourner family also arrived with the Jersey settlers. Oakwood, a simple planter's cottage, (eight miles down the Kingston Road from US 61) has been in their family since 1836 and is now rented to overnight or short-term visitors who want the fantasy of temporarily having a farmstead in the antebellum countryside. Oakwood's biggest plus for history lovers is that the owner, Mrs. Dot Sojourner, is an expert on the legends and lore of the area.

Kingston, Adams County, is off of US 61 about five miles south of Natchez. A historic marker at the intersection of the Kingston Road with the highway offers a thumbnail sketch of the town's history.

Kingston Methodist Church is about 12 miles down the Kingston Road.

Mount Carmel Church is less than a mile down the Mount Carmel Road—turn off the Kingston Road at Egypt Church.

Oakwood is eight miles down the Kingston Road from US 61. Telephone 601-445-4738. Admission fee charged.

Church Hill (or Churchill—both spellings are used) and Christ Church are located on MS 553. From US 61, about eight miles north of Natchez, take the Natchez Trace Parkway for about two miles to the MS 553 exit. The church and store are about six miles ahead.

Accommodations, restaurants and fast food establishments are plentiful in Natchez.

4
Natchez

Poverty and hard times safeguarded antebellum Natchez's legacy to the modern world. The grand houses, the opulent mansions, the fantasies in brick and mortar, at first seemed doomed by the economic rigors that came in the aftermath of the Civil War and the following Reconstruction period. The markets that had once filled the coffers of many local citizens offered little more than survival for years after the war.

During these hard times white columned mansions and antebellum palaces turned stoic weathering faces to the world. Opulent furnishings and family treasures often slipped away to new owners' homes in distant places. Carefully sculpted landscapes dissolved into matted mini-jungles. Making-do evolved into a art. As new fads and styles came into vogue in the rest of the country, old homes were often updated and modernized. But due to a lack of funds, the majority of Natchez's architectural treasures escaped the renovators.

When the first pilgrimages began in the 1930s, so many of the magnificent old homes were unchanged that the annual homes tour grew into a viable year-round business. Today Natchez is a treasure trove of antebellum architecture. The immediate horrors of the Civil War which destroyed so many homes in other parts of the state barely touched Natchez. For the most part the city quietly waited out the war.

In 1863 northern forces headquartered themselves at the mansion Rosalie where they were so gracious as to take up the fine carpets and preserve them for the family. Rosalie, circa 1820, at the foot of South Broadway Street, is located on a bluff above the Mississippi River near the site of the French Fort Rosalie built by Bienville in 1716. The garrison and early settlers were massacred by the Natchez Indians in 1729. The French shortly thereafter wiped out the tribe and continued their dominion of the area until the end of the French and Indian War in 1763 when the English took over. During the American Revolution, in 1779, when the English were occupied elsewhere, the Spanish seized Natchez.

The park adjoining Rosalie on the river bluff is a remnant of the broad esplanade overlooking the river that dominated the Spanish-designed city. Some historians also say that it was once part of Fort Rosalie's parade ground. In the Treaty of San Lorenzo, 1795, Spain and the United States agreed to the 31st parallel as the boundary between the new nation and Spanish territory. On March 30, 1798, the last Spanish officials withdrew from the city.

The public park sits atop Silver Street, Natchez-under-the-hill, the notorious underbelly settlement of earlier times. The river has washed away the scenes of many of the district's sins. The unstable loess bluffs towering above the Under-the-hill Saloon and other establishments may bury the remainder of the street in a mud slide without notice. But until then, this is still the Natchez waterfront and the landing for visiting steamboats.

Back up on Broadway, The Parsonage, a red brick cottage with a white portico, sits on the corner across from Rosalie. This elegant cottage was built to house the mistress of Rosalie's continual stream of visiting preachers. The ladies who guide visitors through Rosalie's Georgian splendor tell of how the builder of the mansion married a pre-adolescent girl in order to "preserve her fortune" after her parents died, then promptly shipped her off to the north and built himself a grand mansion. When she eventually returned, she was seldom without a clergyman at her side, which apparently caused her husband some distress.

One block up from The Parsonage is the Wesley House which curiously blends Steamboat Gothic and Victorian Swiss Chalet. In the next block the lacy iron grillwork on the front galleries of Bontura and its adjoining courtyard are reminiscent of New Orleans and Mobile. Visitors don't have to go far to

Longwood, one of Natchez's most celebrated, eclectic-styled mansions.

experience a wide variety of architectural styles. The Visitor Commission offers a free walking tour map of the old town area. Not to be missed are prime antebellum specimens such as Choctaw, Stanton Hall and Connelly's Tavern on its high mound. Built in Spanish colonial times, the tavern is said to have been frequented by Aaron Burr and his alleged fellow conspirator Herman Blennerhasset.

Burr had relatives in the area. One of the more notable was William Burr Howell, the father of Varina Howell. Varina married Jefferson Davis. She grew up in a rural setting at the Briars on the river bank just south of the modern day bridge (behind the Ramada Inn).

Still in a rural setting, Longwood is the legendary octagonal house that Yankee carpenters abandoned unfinished at the beginning of the war. Their tools and workmanship are on display pretty much as they left them. Dunleith is a classic southern mansion in the Greek temple mode with lush grounds and exotic outbuildings. Monmouth was the home of the hero of the Mexican War, General John Quitman. Melrose preserves much of the opulence of the past in furnishings. Auburn has the most graceful stairwell in town. D'Evereux, said to be named for a Bolivian patriot, surely possesses the most exotic name of any home in town. Natchez mansions come in enough styles, settings and nomenclatures to appeal to almost all tastes.

Natchez is located on US 61 about 70 miles south of Vicksburg. US 98 and US 84 are east/west routes through the city. Accommodations, restaurants and fast food establishments are plentiful.

For a free walking tour map of historic Natchez, lists of all the mansions open for tours and/or bed and breakfast, information on the pilgrimages and other attractions, write the Natchez Convention and Visitor Commission, P.O. Box 794, Natchez, MS 39120-0794. Telephone 800-647-6724 (out of state) or 601-446-6345 (in state).

5

The Other Natchez—
Grand Village
of the Great Sun

Aquaint antebellum town sits on the bluffs above the Mississippi River at Natchez, dreaming of yesterday, unconcerned about tomorrow. This is a quiet place where there's still time to practice the most proper etiquette and reminisce about someone's great-grandmother's trysts and great-grandfather's duels of honor.

There's also another settlement sharing the bluffs, clinging to the underside of the crumbling bank that periodically spills its houses and inhabitants into the river. Natchez-under-the-hill clings to yesterday even more tenaciously than she grips the river's edge. Being naughty has always been the vogue here. Today at least the appearance of being naughty is still very big business, almost as big a business as the antebellum mansions and illusions of opulence are up on the topside of the bluffs.

But there's still another Natchez, one that's not big business, an older, mysterious native Natchez whose first settlements are shrouded in the loess soil that makes up the high rising bluffs on the east side of the Mississippi and its local tributary, St. Catherine's Creek. This Natchez was the seat of government of the Great Sun, supreme ruler of the people who are remembered as Natchez Indians.

The Grand Village of the Great Sun, within the city limits, is surrounded by modern suburbia. Spokespersons at the site of the Mississippi Department of Archives and History's museum and 124-acre National Historic Landmark say, "12,000 to 15,000 years ago, Indians were living here."

Between 1682 and 1729 the Grand Village was a ceremonial center, according to the journals of Frenchmen visiting and living here during those years. Many archaeologists believe the

Woods at the Grand Village of the Great Sun, Natchez.

Natchez culture reached its zenith in the mid-1500s. The native ceremonies the Frenchmen witnessed and wrote about had their roots in pre-historic times.

These early Mississippians were farmers living in scattered settlements, usually on small family farms. They didn't favor tightly clustered villages. The Grand Village of the Great Sun was not an ordinary settlement, but a place of native elegance, where feathers, finery and rituals bonded a people into a nation.

Now centuries have passed and only in imagination can the ancient rituals and ceremonies be played out. Vast empty green spaces separate the mounds that once were pedestals for palaces and temples, the only sounds are wild birds calling to each other across the grassy rises. The soil, the dissolving loess bluffs, shifting and gliding over centuries of raindrops to do their cover work, shelter the tangible mementos of the Natchez. Deep under the ground artifacts of the Natchez are still safe. The earth chooses to safeguard an eclectic mixture of household, personal and ritual items. The journals of the French adventurers and early colonists give us intangible clues, and in some cases drawings of the Natchez lifestyle.

The visitor's center displays drawings and artifacts. An entrance way approached under an arbor of wisteria leads to the museum area, plus offices, a theatre and a gift shop. A natural thicket of native trees separates the parking lot and center from the wide flat expanses of the plazas from which the mounds rise. The mound of the Great Sun's house is near the center stage of the complex. Here was the palace of the king. Here the male ruler of a matrilineal society resided with his wives and retainers. When he died his house was burned, the mound raised a few more feet and then the house of his successor erected. The next king was the eldest son of the dead Sun's sister and he was required to marry commoners. Commoners in that society were called "stinkards" which is probably the most interesting descriptive sentiment any elitist group has ever come up with for the general citizenry.

The Tattooed Serpent, brother to the Great Sun, presided as chief priest at the temple mound to the far right of the compound. The temple housed the bones of previous Great

Choctaw children on a visit to the Grand Village of the Great Sun, Natchez.

Suns and was the scene of funeral rites when a Great Sun died. Upon the king's death his wives and retainers were strangled in an elaborate ceremony so that they might accompany him into the next life. A sacred perpetual fire burned in the temple's inner sanctum, symbolic of the Sun from which the royal family had descended. Special attendants maintained the fire. If it went out, they lost their lives.

To the left of the plazas in the shade of the forest is a recreated Natchez thatched-roof farm house and corn crib. This would have been a stinkard homestead. In the shadowy interior, the simplicity of an ancient culture is recaptured and conjured back to reality. The faded pages of the Frenchmen's journals, the circles of ancient house timbers, and charcoals of long extinguished fires covered by the protective arms of the Natchez's own mother earth attest to the authenticity. There is a representative garden of peppers, squash, beans and corn near the cottage.

The staff inside the visitor's center can answer most any questions visitors might have about the Natchez and what became of them. Basically their friendship with the French dissolved into hostilities that resulted in massacres and atrocities. Eventually the last Great Sun was captured by the French, sold into slavery at New Orleans, and shipped out to the Dominican Republic where the harsh tropical climate, and the harsher life of a field hand proved more than he could bear and he died.

According to historians some small fragments of the Natchez tribe escaped into the wilds of Louisiana, while others made it to the safety of their Chickasaw allies' camps to the northeast, where they slowly dissolved into that people.

The Grand Village is located in the city of Natchez. To get there take US 61 South to Jefferson Davis Boulevard. Follow the signs. The boulevard ends in a cul-de-sac beside the Grand Village entrance gate. Admission free.

Special education programs are available for school and adult groups. Address: The Grand Village of the Natchez, 400 Jefferson Davis Boulevard, Natchez, MS 39120. Telephone 601-446-6502.

Accommodations, restaurants and fast food establishments are plentiful in Natchez. The Grand Village has picnic facilities and restrooms.

6
Washington—Jefferson College

When Mississippi was largely wilderness, a wild frontier that intimidated mild-mannered men, this town offered some hope for a more genteel lifestyle. Jefferson Military College located here still retains the look and feel of that time, an appearance of European elegance transported to the wilderness in its Georgian buildings and surrounding forest. Sometimes from outside the school's white wooden fence, peering through the wispy strands of Spanish moss hanging from the ancient sprawling oaks lining the streets, visitors might well think they have found the threshold of a time warp.

The venerable old school, where classes were suspended in 1964 after more than 150 years, has become not only a museum, a historic landmark, a movie and television setting, but an actor in its own right. In the television mini-series *North and South,* Jefferson College portrays West Point, the U.S. Military Academy as it was in the early 1800s. But no fictional role could ever compare for sheer adventure, historical background and glamour to Jefferson College's role in real life.

Founded in 1802 by an act of the First General Assembly of the Mississippi Territory, the school was named in honor of President Thomas Jefferson.

Out under the campus' massive oaks, Aaron Burr, former vice president of the United States, was arraigned on charges of treason. Disputed legends claim the young boy Jefferson Davis was a student here and the artist and naturalist John James Audubon was a drawing teacher. Mississippi's own premier naturalist Benjamin Wailes' tenure here is documented.

A sample of the type of woodland wonder that inspired Wailes can be found along the campus Nature Trail that winds

Jefferson College, Washington.

through the woods, passing St. Catherine's Creek, the college
cemetery and Ellicott Springs. Surveyor Andrew Ellicott
camped here in 1797 just prior to his expedition to survey the
31st parallel which determined the boundary between the U.S.
and Spanish West Florida.

Today the college and the town of Washington along US 61,
six miles northeast of Natchez, rewards travelers who make a
stop and linger a while with a sense of Mississippi's past
unavailable elsewhere. This town was once the territorial capital
of Mississippi.

After Jefferson College, Washington's most notable historic
institution was probably the Methodist church, where the first
state constitutional convention met in July 1817. According to

local legends this Methodist church was the first brick church erected in what was then known as the Southwest Territory.

Historic markers, along US 61 within the Washington city limit signs, make the college easy to find. Interpretive markers also designate the college President's House and the church site. Reversals of financial circumstances and simple neglect have taken their toll on many historic structures in the area. But you only need a dash of imagination to see the volatile general of the Tennessee Volunteers, Andrew Jackson, and his troops camped out here in a false alarm call-up prior to the War of 1812. You need only walk across the vast expanses of lawn at Jefferson College, wander through the empty halls, linger by the well, stop in the garden on a quiet Mississippi morning to capture a fleeting glimmer of that distant yesterday when the hero of the battle of New Orleans, his beloved wife, Rachel, and their adopted son Andrew Jackson, Jr., were regaled here before traveling home to Nashville on the Natchez Trace.

One of the sights most common to the young cadets in the early days of the school had to be the parade of "Kaintucks" walking past the school towards their homes in the north. The Kaintucks were the boatmen who rode flat-bottomed rafts through a maze of inland waterways to the Mississippi and on to New Orleans. After delivering farm produce and manufactured goods to the city, the boatmen were paid in gold and headed up river to Natchez where they could take an overland route home, rather than fight their way back over the currents of the rivers. Until about 1820 when the steamboats began to ply the Mississippi, the homeward-bound boatmen opted for the arduous trail dubbed the "Trace" by early French explorers.

As the rough-hewn Kaintucks passed the prim, manicured parade grounds of red brick Jefferson College, they were leaving civilization behind and walking into a world of barbarian murderers and an unsympathetic forest. But the world of Jefferson College and its refined young gentlemen cadets was probably just as alien. A museum on the grounds documents the cadets' schooling. Throughout the year a basketmaker demonstrates his craft on the campus. Local programs and activities are frequently held in the old school buildings.

Jefferson College is located on US 61 about six miles northeast of Natchez and about two miles southwest of the southernmost reaches of the Natchez Trace Parkway. Admission free.

The grounds are open from sunup to sundown and the buildings are open from 9 a.m. to 5 p.m. except Sunday when they are open from 1 p.m. to 5 p.m. There are restrooms in the museum. For more information contact Jefferson College, P.O. Box 100, Washington, MS 39190. Telephone 601-441-2901.

Accommodations, restaurants and fast food establishments are plentiful in Natchez.

7
The Natchez Trace Parkway—Below Jackson

The Natchez Trace Parkway stretches diagonally across Mississippi, cuts a corner across northwest Alabama, then darts into Tennessee. The Trace ran straight through the heart of frontier America and some of the juiciest legends of our nation's beginnings.

Today, the parkway allows travelers to explore the reality, the myths, the legends, the ghost towns and the forests along the ancient road by car. Roughly paralleling the Old Trace, the parkway stretches for more than 400 miles from the Natchez area to the Duck River in Tennessee. The National Park Service administers the parkway and has plans to eventually have it run about 450 miles from Natchez to Nashville.

Markers along the route tell the tales of battles, disasters, triumphs and survival. Cypress swamps, ghost towns, Indian encampments and ancient pre-Columbian mounds can be explored just a few steps from the roadway. The Trace follows prehistoric bison and game routes. Archaeologists say the road was old when the walls of Jericho were being built. Conservative estimates claim settlements at Natchez stretch back 12,000 to 15,000 years. Those early native residents would have used the Trace. The ancient road is populated by a thousand memories of enterprising Indians, bold warriors, Spanish Conquistadors, French explorers, British colonists, American militia men, adventurers and "land pirates."

The fledgling United States of America started mail service down the Trace in 1800, sending dispatches from Washington, D.C., through Nashville to the far southwestern corner of the nation at Natchez. The post riders, an early version of the Pony Express, became so influential on the Trace that their symbolized image was chosen by the U.S. Park Service to represent the parkway. Travelers often waited for the post rider to leave for Nashville so they could travel in the company of someone who was well acquainted with the route.

If you are ready to begin a journey across the grain of America's history, this is the place to start. A section of the old Trace beckons like a tunnel through the wild matted forest at the beginning of the parkway directly off of US 61 north of Natchez. In the quiet canopied world over the ancient dirt road bed, a tenacious sunbeam breaks through the green roof; in the dust the tracks of the wild animals who roam at will through the parkway make the distant shouts and songs of the travelers, the boatmen, the "Kaintucks" come almost within earshot.

After landing on the Natchez waterfront from New Orleans where they had sold their produce, manufactured goods and often the flatboats that had brought them south on a maze of inland waterways, the boatmen's first order of business was to buy supplies and foodstuff for the journey while they waited for a sizable company of like-minded travelers to assemble. They probably, also, took time to read the wanted posters and reward notices for bandits operating on the Trace.

Though the journey would take the northward bound travelers across the frontiers of two Indian nations, the Indians were usually the least of their worries. White men staining their skins with berry juice and dressing in buckskins, in an attempt to pass as Indians, lurked along the Trace to rob and kill travelers at will. The parkway is so lightly traveled today that at some dense woodland thicket, you might easily imagine the ghosts of the bandits are still lurking, ready to waylay travelers.

Emerald Mound, 10.3 miles along the route, had slipped into the haze of pre-history by the time of the bandits and boatmen. Archaeologists speculate it was built about 1300 by kinsmen of the Creek, Choctaw and Natchez Indians. It covers nearly eight acres and is just the first of many ceremonial and houehold mounds of ancient people along the Trace.

Mount Locust, 15.5 miles into the Parkway, is a recreated stand, a frontier inn, that displays some of the better quarters offered to travelers during the early 1800s. Established in the

The Natchez Trace was a tunnel through the forest for early American travelers.

1700s, Mount Locust began as a primitive frontier plantation. The owner, like other stand operators, took in travelers to supplement his income. A park ranger stationed here will tell you a version of Mount Locust's and the Trace's story. You can walk up on the porches and peek in at the modest pioneer furnishings. The stands were attractive not so much for their accommodations as they were as a place where travelers could join the company of a few additional human beings to help ward off the demons of the night. Darkness brought the screams of panthers and other sounds of horror. So many bears were killed along the Trace that their numbers seem phenomenal.

Wild turkeys, red fox, coyotes and deer are common sights even now. The fiercest predators have vanished into the same ghostly realms as towns such as Rocky Springs. At the 54.8 mile marker, this ghost town is a relic of the cotton kingdom. A short walk from the parkway, along well laid-out and marked paths, takes visitors into a world of deeply eroded gullies—land that cotton spoiled. There is the rubble of homes and stores. The climate doesn't preserve many artifacts left in the open, but there is an abandoned safe with curious trees growing through its doors, cement cisterns and well-heads. Shrouded in Spanish moss, a cemetery with its antique tombstones cracked and broken waits for the final reckoning. A red brick Methodist church remains intact, the only building to survive.

Sixty-one miles into the modern parkway, travelers cross the Lower Choctaw Boundary which was the dividing line between the earliest settled parts of Mississippi and the Choctaw Indians' land. Passports were required to cross through the Choctaw and Chickasaw nations in frontier times. And the Indians retained the right to operate all stands and ferries in their nations, but many of the inn-keepers were actually Indian-white mixed-bloods. The sites of stands, along with their particular legends, are recorded on markers all along the parkway.

If a traveler escaped the ravages of nature, waded the swamps, swam the streams, climbed the hills, survived exposure to the elements, poisonous snakes and wild animals by the time he reached the Choctaw boundary, he would be at least relatively free of bandits until he reached the far side of the Chickasaw nation in Tennessee, where more white hoodlum gangs waited.

No deep South trip would be complete without a visit or two to sites of Civil War battles. The most notable site marked on the Trace south of Jackson is the Battle of Raymond at the 78.3 mile post. This battle was part of the infamous Vicksburg campaign.

The Natchez Trace Parkway entrance is about eight miles north of Natchez on US 61. There are ample exits along the 70-or-so-mile route to Jackson. The parkway is administered and policed by the National Park Service, U.S. Department of the Interior. Speed limit is 50 mph. Trucks are prohibited. Admission free.

Allowing ample time for sightseeing and exploring, the entire parkway can be driven comfortably in two days, making it an ideal adventure for a family with a few days for a holiday. Individual segments can be explored on shorter trips. The lower Trace from near Natchez to Jackson can be leisurely explored in a day or less.

Frequent rest stops with clean modern restroom facilities are provided all along the route as well as picnic areas in picturesque settings alongside streams and in forest glades. There is a campground at Rocky Springs. Fast food establishments, restaurants and overnight accommodations can best be found at Jackson or Natchez. There are no service stations on the parkway below Jackson.

For camping fees and regulations or other information, contact Superintendent, Natchez Trace Parkway, Rural Route 1, NT-143, Tupelo, MS 38801. Telephone 601-842-1572.

8

The Natchez Trace Parkway—Above Jackson

The Natchez Trace Parkway's run to Tennessee is interrupted at Jackson. The southern portion of the road ends at I-20 here. Approximately 20 miles across I-220 to I-55 north of the city, the parkway is resumed. The serenity of the forested land along the meandering roadway is a welcome retreat from the modern superhighways.

Less than a mile after re-entering the parkway, the Mississippi Crafts Center's log cabin eagerly greets visitors with bright flags snapping above its deep green woodland setting. Mississippi-made rocking chairs, quilts and toys are displayed on the porch. Inside, the intricate designs of Choctaw baskets and other Native American crafts vie with white-pioneer-styled pottery, quilts, carvings, toys and furniture for the shopper's attention. The Crafts Center is operated by the Mississippi Craftsmen's Guild, a group organized to preserve and promote the folk and traditional crafts of the state. Some members also pursue contemporary crafts. But for the history lover the guild's frequent demonstrations of basket making, quilting, spinning, weaving, wood carving, the making of musical instruments, and even pioneer-styled cooking (there's an outdoor "beehive" oven on the grounds) offer a view of the pragmatic skills necessary for a community in earlier times. (The gift shop could supply the answers to the most perplexing questions of Christmas or birthday gift giving.)

A few miles further up the parkway at milepost 104.5, the Old Trace beckons travelers to stretch their legs and take a sample walk along the path frontier adventurers followed. This is also near the site of Brashears' Stand. Turner Brashears advertised his inn to travelers leaving Natchez in 1806 as "a house of entertainment in the wilderness."

The parkway hugs the shore of the Ross Barnett Reservoir as it makes its way to the Boyd Mounds (milepost 106.9) which are thought to have been used by different Native American groups as burial sites. The West Florida Boundary, as drawn at the close of the French and Indian War (The Seven Years War) in 1763, is at milepost 107.9. The exotic world of the Cypress Swamp is easily penetrable at milepost 122. An elevated walkway guides visitors through the timeless world of the southern swamp's plant community.

The secrets of the past waiting to be revealed, the scenic beauty of the unspoiled wilderness interspersed with the lazy, sprawling rich fields of corn and cotton beside the roadway wrap travelers in an idyllic aura. The poetry of place names— Yockanookany, Red Dog, Witch Dance—set an imaginative rhythm of native words and thoughts.

French Camp marries the memory of white pioneer skills with a Native American legend. At milepost 180.7 a sorghum mill is the site of syrup-making each autumn. An authentic dogtrot-styled cabin dating from pioneer days has been moved onto the site as a reception center. On the old Trace the inn of Louis LeFleur made this a welcomed stop. LeFleur was the father of the Choctaw chief Greenwood Leflore.

Less than ten miles up the Parkway at milepost 193.9, the Jeff Busby Picnic Area boasts one of the highest points in Mississippi at 603 feet. The height of the overlook can be best appreciated after a cold front has moved through the area and pushed out the haze that usually obscures panoramic views. A nature trail here offers a 20-minute walk where native plants and their uses as food and medicines by white pioneers is chronicled.

The Trace is testimony to Mississippi's rich Indian history. Hernando De Soto and his expedition were probably the first post-Columbian white men to pass over a portion of the Trace (which had several different arteries in those days), and a marker at milepost 243.3 claims the former Conquistador, a cohort of Pizarro, and his party spent the winter "near here" in 1540–41. The Chickasaw Council House Picnic Area is at milepost 251.1. Pontatok, the capital of the Chickasaw nation

French Camp on the Natchez Trace was originally settled by Louis LeFleur, father of Choctaw chief Greenwood Leflore.

in the 1820s, was nearby. At milepost 261.8 a Chickasaw village's site is open for exploration.

The Tupelo headquarters of the parkway, milepost 266, has a visitor's center with a museum displaying Indian artifacts, including pre-Columbian pieces, found along the Trace. There is also a collection of memorabilia from the Euro-Americans who started using the Indian roads about 1700. Regular showings of a movie dramatically tell the Trace's story. The ghosts, scalawags, bandits and cut-throats who once hampered travel for good citizens and valiant heros steal the show.

Indian sites and natural features are highlighted all the way to the Alabama border. The parkway continues through Alabama up into Tennessee. Some travelers may want to extend their journey all the way to the end of the Trace and on to Nashville to visit the home of one of the great heros of the frontier Trace, Andrew Jackson. Jackson not only traveled the Trace for business and military purposes, he and his bride Rachel Robards made a trip up the Trace shortly after their marriage (in southwest Mississippi) that could be called a "honeymoon." Later, when the date and validity of Rachel's divorce from her first husband was questioned, testimony from fellow-travelers during that Trace journey was sought by political enemies to prove Jackson less than honorable for having slept "under the same blanket" with another man's wife.

By 1820 steamboats on the Mississippi and other waterways made travel on the Trace impractical. Gradually the road dissolved into local byways and forgotten tunnels through the forest only to spring back to life temporarily during the Civil War to facilitate both Federal and Confederate troop movements. In 1909 the Mississippi Chapter of the Daughters of the American Revolution began a campaign to mark the old Trace. Their work has climaxed in the parkway.

The upper Trace entrance at Jackson is from I-55 North. Speed limit is 50 mph. Trucks are prohibited. Admission free.

Overnight accommodations, fast food establishments, restaurants and service stations are best found in Jackson and Tupelo, though ample exits from the parkway point the way to lodging, food and gas. The Jeff Busby Picnic Area, located about 90 miles from Jackson, contains campsites, a camp store and the only service station on the parkway.

An abundance of picnic areas and rest stop facilities, with clean modern restrooms, make the Natchez Trace Parkway an easy journey for families with young children.

For more information contact Superintendent, Natchez Trace Parkway, Rural Route 1, NT-143, Tupelo, MS 38801. Telephone 601-842-1572.

9
Port Gibson

Port Gibson is a city of contrasts. Trees form green canopies over streets meandering past antebellum homes oozing nostalgia. The business district still has a flourish of wrought iron balconies, and in the wavy vapors of heat rising off the distant pavement, it is easy to imagine that you are getting only a slightly blurred vision of the past.

General U.S. Grant made this town a major objective in his 1863 campaign to capture Vicksburg, according to the local history experts. They say the battle for Port Gibson exhibited all the features of a major amphibious operation and that there were tactical lessons in the local battles that American military forces had to relearn in World War II.

But the thing most people remember about General Grant and his sojourn in and around Port Gibson, is that when the victory was his, he departed from the normal scorched earth policy and proclaimed the town "too beautiful to burn."

Port Gibson probably best lives up to the grand expectations such statements as Grant's historical pronouncement generate in the springtime when the azaleas and dogwoods are in full bloom. That is the time the local Chamber of Commerce promotes tourism with a pilgrimage. During the pilgrimage many grand and unique homes are open for leisurely tours. But if you can't make the spring pilgrimage and just absolutely yearn to see the state's oldest formal garden, awe-inspiring spiral staircases, chandeliers from the steamboat Robert E. Lee, or the front porch where Henry Clay once addressed local citizens, you can make arrangements through the Port Gibson-Claiborne County Chamber of Commerce to tour a wide assortment of antebellum homes and buildings by appointment any time of year.

The Chamber of Commerce offices and tourist headquarters are located in the Samuel Gibson House, circa 1805, the oldest surviving house in town. The Gibson House, which is sort of a combination of cabin-cottage, was moved in 1980 from its original location to its present site on Church Street, which is the main highway (US 61) through town. The building has undergone a historical rehabilitation, and visitors will want to stop here not only to see the house but to pick up brochures, maps and other information on the area as well. The Chamber offers maps to three self-guided automobile tours of the area. You can pick one that suits your schedule and interests.

The maps for the self-guided tours are the key to discovering and exploring the city's contrasting images. From the idyllic town, full of so many houses of worship, it has been called "a city of churches," head north up US 61/Church Street. St. Joseph's Catholic Church, c. 1849, is the oldest surviving church building in town. Temple Gemiluth Chessed with its squat onion domes is a 19th century Jewish house of worship. The Presbyterian Church announces its presence with a giant, golden-gilded hand pointed heavenward. Turn west on Walnut Street and follow the signs to Grand Gulf. The nuclear power station where history is being made looms ahead. Stop at the visitors center for information on touring the plant. A few years ago a tornado whipped through the grounds of the power station and took a chunk out of one of the high chimneys of a cooling tower. Before it was repaired the jagged edge made a chilling contrast with the town's golden hand pointing towards heaven. The contrast between the ultra modern domed reactor houses, the cooling towers, and the quaint town wed to yesteryear is staggering even with the intact cooling tower.

Four miles south of Port Gibson a scenic overlook on Bayou Pierre, near the junction with the marked portion of MS 552, has a log replica of one of the first Presbyterian church buildings in the state, called a "preaching stand." The small cabin sits on a hill side that in winter offers a panoramic view of the Grand Gulf nuclear station and surrounding farms.

And then there's Windsor. It is located 12 miles southwest of Port Gibson. The twisting dusty road that brings you across the

fields from MS 552 to the old home site is authentically
reminiscent of times past. Twenty-three columns ravaged by a
fire that destroyed the grand house have been further vandalized
by time. A tenant farmer's cabin, meager and modest to the
point of desperation in the best of times, now riddled with age,
stands sentinel by the elegant columns. The contrast seems
overly symbolic. Mark Twain, once a pilot on the river, said he
used the observatory atop Windsor as a landmark. Col. Sam
Magruder, whose mother was a nine-year-old visiting her
grandparents at Windsor the night it burned, remembers Eliz-
abeth Taylor visited the ruins and a made-for-the-movies
cemetery out front in an epic movie of the 1950s, *Raintree
County*.

Continue on MS 552 south of Windsor and almost immediately you can take the rough unpaved road to the site of
Bruinsburg, an early river town and site of Civil War activities.
This road should only be attempted in dry weather. A short
distance further down 552 is the Windsor Battlefield, another
site of Civil War action. Indian mounds can be seen along the
road in this area. Further down 552 is Alcorn State University.
This was one of the first land grant college for blacks in the
nation, established in 1871. Oakland Chapel on the campus is a
significant example of Greek Revival architecture in temple
form. Steps and railings from Windsor have been incorporated
into the chapel. The chapel is a survivor from an earlier
institution, Oakland College, established in 1830.

From Alcorn follow the signs on the dirt road going west to
Rodney. Just a few miles beyond Port Gibson, Rodney was a
thriving river town in the early 1800's. Today it is a ghost
town. A shift in the course of the Mississippi River away from
Rodney caused a slow emigration from the town. The folks at
the Port Gibson Chamber warn that the road to Rodney is so
bad (no matter what the weather) that only the determined
should follow it.

South on US 61 about ten miles out of Port Gibson, the
"Old Country Store," a general store, caters to the local
plantation trade much as it did when it was established in 1875.
The store offers exotic bits of Mississippiana for sale as well as

Ruins of the grand house Windsor near Port Gibson.

the ice cream and soft drinks that make life on a summer's day almost tolerable. There is a free museum in the store. The store itself could fall into the folk museum category.

Port Gibson is also very near the Natchez Trace Parkway, and such Trace spots as Grindstone Ford, Mangum Mound, Rocky Springs (a ghost town), and a section of the old Trace worn deep into the earth. The ancient Trace roadway, the modern country roads and US 61 round out the studies in contrast the area offers.

Port Gibson is located on US 61 about 44 miles north of Natchez and 26 miles south of Vicksburg.

Some accommodations are available in town, others at Natchez and Vicksburg. Restaurants are scarce. Picnickers can find quiet, idyllic spots on the Natchez Trace Parkway.

For free maps, brochures and other information contact Port Gibson-Claiborne County Chamber of Commerce, P.O. Box 491, Port Gibson, MS 39150. Telephone 601-437-4351.

10

Grand Gulf Military Monument Park

Grand Gulf, a place of wildwoods and rampant under-growth, watches the Mississippi River regularly spill across the flat fields at the base of its loess hills. In the early spring, acres of wild mustard bloom, sending thick, broad yellow streaks through the green meadows while blue skies reflect on the muddy water creating an illusion of an enchanted lake. This is a place intent on swallowing up all semblances of man-made reality.

The hungry grasses nibble away at the edges of the narrow road twisting its way through the old town site. A half dozen or so buildings, ghostly, weathered and mostly uninhabited, are the sole survivors of this ghost town.

Named for the whirlpool, or gulf, formed by the current of the Mississippi surging against a large rock, Grand Gulf was settled by the French in the 1700s. But the settlement remained a small outpost until the cotton planters discovered its convenient location on the river. A proper town was laid out in 1828 and Grand Gulf was incorporated in 1833. Cotton came down the Big Black River from as far away as Jackson for transshipment on the Mississippi. A railroad ran to the cotton wharves. For two decades Grand Gulf is said to have shipped more cotton than any other port in the state. The population grew to about 1000. The town had two newspapers, a hospital, a school, churches of several denominations, plus numerous stores and businesses. Touring theatrical companies came via the steamboats bringing an element of sophistication to the river town. "Grog shops" are said to have been plentiful. Perhaps those shops' goods fueled the desire for the duels which were fought out on the river's sandbars.

Disaster seemed to have been the town's most frequent visitor. A yellow fever epidemic in 1843 claimed the lives of many citizens. Ten years later a tornado ravaged the place. But the worse disaster came when the Mississippi turned on the town. Between 1855 and 1860 the river gobbled up 55 city blocks. By the outbreak of the Civil War, the population had been reduced to 158 people.

But fate was not through with Grand Gulf. Disaster made several more visits. Union forces occupied the area twice. As they withdrew the second time, they burned what remained of the town.

Grand Gulf Military Monument Park is a 400-acre area that ties together the memory of the town, the mystique of the war and the relics of both.

The park museum's Civil War collections include uniforms, guns, bloodstained sashes, letters, diaries and newspapers. The letters are from both Union and Confederate backers and soldiers. (One Union soldier wrote home of his amazement that the local people would abandon their possessions and flee before the advancing Union forces.) An extensive collection of carriages, wagons and other 19th century conveyances are housed in a separate building.

Several of the buildings on the grounds have been moved into the park from other locations. A straight-square dogtrot was once a Confederate general's headquarters. A working waterwheel-gristmill has been placed on a pond. A Carpenter Gothic architectural masterpiece, once a Catholic church at Rodney, another ghost town downstream, now crowns a knoll near the park's entrance.

Fort Wade is located near the park entrance and Fort Coburn is located a few miles upstream, but is easily reached by automobile. Both forts saw intense action during the Civil War.

The old Grand Gulf cemetery is within the park, high on a hill near the park's observation tower. From the top of the tower you can see the Mississippi snake its way pass the bits of land General Grant's armies fought so tenaciously to control. The old Spanish House near Fort Wade is a typical homestead of Mississippi's earliest white settlers. Across the road from the

A Carpenter-Gothic architecture masterpiece, the Rodney Catholic Church has been relocated to Grand Gulf Military Park.

park, a boardwalk leads to the river's edge where visitors can get a close up view of the river and the modern tugs pushing barges pass the memories of Grand Gulf.

Grand Gulf Military Monument Park is about seven miles northeast of Port Gibson and US 61 on the Grand Gulf Road. Admission to the park is free, but a small fee is charged for admission to the main museum/gift shop. There are camping and RV facilities within the park, as well as restrooms.

Picnic facilities are ample. Nearest accommodations and restaurants are at Port Gibson.

For more information contact Grand Gulf Military Monument Park, Route 2, Box 389, Port Gibson, MS 39150. Telephone 601-437-5911.

11
Vicksburg National Military Park

Vicksburg is forever locked in the grips of the Civil War. The Union soldiers buried in the National Cemetery here and the Confederate soldiers sleeping until eternity in the City Cemetery have become part of the very earth that is Vicksburg. Even if we forget, both armies will still be here holding their last positions.

But we aren't likely to forget. Vicksburg National Military Park's 1,800 acres of hills, woodlands and high river bluffs have sixteen miles of roadways lined with epic memorials. This is a park of giant ambitions, grandiose ideals and quiet memories preserved in stone and bronze. Horses still dash into battle, cannons still stand at the ready, rifles are still aimed, wounded soldiers still bleed, their cries shaped by the artisans' hands so our hearts will never fail to hear. Union generals sit straight and tall on great bronze horses—larger than life. Confederate generals wave their swords towards the heavens in emotional displays.

Monuments and memorials have been built by the states who sent soldiers to the battle. Illinois, Indiana, Ohio, Michigan, Minnesota, Tennessee, Missouri, Mississippi, Alabama, Texas, Louisiana—the list goes on. You can drive the 16-mile tour, or if you are particularly energetic and don't mind the heat in summer, you can walk or jog.

You will want to begin your tour of the park at the visitor's center at the main entrance.

The license plates on cars in the parking lot read like a roster of states—Alaska, Illinois, Michigan, California, Iowa, Texas, Georgia. Each year over 1.5 million people from all over the country visit the park. A large number of the visitors stop to

A Confederate Memorial, Vicksburg National Military Park.

converse with park officials at the center's front desk, to tell
them they had relatives who fought here. If you enjoy eaves-
dropping, browse at the book rack near the front desk. Perhaps
the most enlightening bit of information to be gathered is that a
large number of northerners seem to have as much interest in
"the war" as southerners.

A large sign in the lobby reads, "Remember it is 1863." The
rumble of distant cannon fire never ceases. A 18-minute-long
movie exploring the whys and wherefores of the battle here in
this Mississippi River town, called the Gibraltar of the Confederacy, is shown on the hour and half hour throughout the
day. There is a mini-museum in the center. Here you can hear
the re-created voices of a doctor's wife, a Confederate major and

a Union sergeant read from their diaries, written during the terrible time of the 47-day siege that climaxed in the fall of the city. Replicas of the caves the citizens of the town dug into the bluffs and the hills for shelter from Union bombardment give a realistic representation of the dust and dirt that dominated everyday life. A short walk outside the center on a summer's day will introduce you to an authentic dose of the humidity and heat the armies and the citizens endured.

But even on the hottest days going outside is a wonderful adventure because of the "living history" re-enactments. Soldiers fire their muskets at 9, 10 and 11 a.m. and at 2 and 3 p.m. each day except Monday and Tuesday. Cannon drill is at 9:30 a.m. and 1:30 p.m. and cannon firings at 10:30 a.m. and 2:30 p.m. (except Monday and Tuesday) from early spring through the end of August.

With the boom of the "real-thing" ringing in your ears, you don't need another sign announcing, "Remember, it is 1863 and the siege is in progress."

In the visitor's center request a map of the park for a self-guided tour. There are guides available for about $10. But with the map, and the background the movie and museum provide, you can enjoy touring and understanding the significance of the battle and the park at your own pace.

Within the park is the Vicksburg National Cemetery and the iron-clad gunboat "Cairo." The Cairo is now moored in a permanent drydock and has its own museum overlooking the Yazoo River near where it joins the Mississippi. The Cairo, a Union gunboat, would be worth a visit all by itself.

The Cairo was headed up the Yazoo to destroy Confederate batteries when it became the first vessel in history to be sunk by an electrically detonated mine. Her wartime record might have been dubious but the Cairo has become precious to historians because of what went down with her when she sank. Preserved, in time-capsule form, information about naval construction, naval stores, armament and the personal gear of the crewmen who served on board document the life and times of the gunboat. The vast array of artifacts recovered from the Cairo before and after it was salvaged in the early 1960s is on display in the museum. These items and the gunboat itself offer a slightly different perspective on the Civil War.

Vicksburg National Military Park, located on US 80 (Clay Street) in Vicksburg, is open every day of the year except Christmas. The Visitor's Center is open from 8 a.m. to 5 p.m. A leisurely tour of the park, Visitor's Center, the Cairo and the National Cemetery can take the better part of a day. There are some picnic facilities in the park and lots of fast food places just beyond the entrance. Accommodations, restaurants and fast food establishments are numerous in Vicksburg.

The park is operated by the National Park Service. Admission fee charged. For more information on Vicksburg National Military Park and Cemetery, write Superintendent, P. O. Box 349, 3201 Clay Street, Vicksburg, MS 39180. Telephone 601-636-0583.

12
Vicksburg, the City

The Spirit of Vicksburg plies the muddy waters of the Yazoo Diversion Canal, on a course followed by the Mississippi River until 1876. The shore line is thick with willows, a green jungle where only the most filtered light ever touches the ground. The excursion boat passes the ruins of the sternwheeler Sprague marooned on a bank. Up the Yazoo the captain-narrator points out the heights that once sheltered the Spanish Los Nogales, and later the American Walnut Hills, before the settlements in the area became known as Vicksburg. The same heights, now within the Vicksburg National Military Park, were crowned by Fort Hill, the strategic prize that caused Union forces to lay seize to this "Gibralter of the Confederacy" during the Civil War.

Once U. S. Grant's forces even conspired to cut a diversion path for the Mississippi so Union troops could bypass the terrible guns that roared from the city's heights. Ironically, nature eventually made her own cut more than ten years after the war ended. In the meantime General Grant had to resort to other tactics.

One of his first maneuvers was to have Admiral David Farragut's forces sail up the river and bombard the city. Today one of the highpoints of the city's skyline is the old Warren County Courthouse, circa 1857, now the Court House Museum. The gunboats enjoyed using the prominent landmark for target practice until the Confederates turned the courthouse into a prison for their Union prisoners of war. This ploy is credited with saving the building.

Back on the river the smell of wilderness, of damp earth in unpolluted places, the scent of rain pelting dry land is the

Courthouse Museum, Vicksburg.

prevailing aroma. Nature has conspired with the tour operators to beautify the shoreline with natural growth to the north of the landing. De Soto Island directly across from the city, lying between the diversion canal and the river, once known as De Soto Point, was a choice spot for duels.

Dueling was a favorite sport of early Vicksburg, even though it was illegal. De Soto Point was Louisiana territory, out of the reach of Mississippi authorities and too far removed from law enforcement officers of the other state to pose a threat to prospective duelers. One local legend tells of the mistress of Lakemont (a house at the corner of Main and Adams Streets) who spilled a bottle of jasmine-like perfume when a servant came to warn of an impending duel between the lady's husband and a political opponent. The mistress of Lakemont raced to an upper story veranda with her opera glasses and watched the entire drama of her husband's demise. Later the upper stories of the house burned. But even today at Lakemont people claim to smell her perfume and see her shadowy presence in the back garden. Once during a pilgrimage tour a giant antique mirror cracked, with a loud resounding noise, for no apparent reason. Many people have interpreted this as a message from the "perfumed lady," but exactly what the message meant is not clear.

The excursion boat turns around and comes back up the island shoreline before venturing out into the current of the Mississippi on its presently preferred route. Evening time dinner-excursions run out into the Mississippi sunset, but in the daytime, the boat turns back for the landing near the massive bridges stretching to Louisiana. Antique cannons still guard the hillsides along the river front. Several industrial enterprises between the bridges and the landing keep the journey from becoming too prosaic.

The prim red brick, white portico train depot near the landing, houses a concession offering a "visual" interpretation of the battle for the city. Levee Street, above the landing, ran out to Catfish Row, the legendary spot where many claimed the Delta ended. Catfish Row is gone now, as are the notorious groups of gamblers who made their living in the region around Levee Street.

Vicksburg, founded by a preacher, didn't immediately opt for the high road culturally. Many citizens preferred a rowdier lifestyle than the ruling gentry would allow. A war against the gamblers is said to have started when one of their number disrupted a Fourth of July picnic. He was promptly tarred-and-feathered by the good citizens and warned to leave town. When his cohorts protested and in a resulting scuffle one of the gentry's own number was shot and killed, the good citizens post haste hung five of the gamblers. Their bodies were left dangling overnight as a warning to others of their persuasion.

Gambling was not the only dangerous profession in pre-Civil War Vicksburg. Newspaper editors there had remarkably short lives. At least five editors were fatally gunned down in duels, two were wounded, one committed suicide and one was sent to jail. The editors' demise and misfortunes were brought about by the political rivalry of two local newspapers, the *Sentinel* and the *Whig*.

Gunfights in the streets of the river town were not uncommon. And even the backdrop of some of the streets, such as Openwood, still suggest a wild west atmosphere.

But there were some citizens engaged in the more mundane pursuits of commerce and professional prowess. They built elegant townhouses, traveled to Europe, educated their sons in the East and pursued what they deemed more noble ambitions. Then the Civil War erupted. From April 12, 1861, to April 9, 1865, fighting raged across the South.

Those elegant townhouses of the lost gentry best tell the story of the city and the citizens' struggle for survival. Cedar Grove's (2200 Oak Street) front door was ripped open by a cannon ball. After all these years the door of the opulent house has only been patched. And in the front parlor, a cannon ball firmly lodged in the wall has been left in place as a reminder of the barrage the homes of the city endured. This particular home belonged to a gentleman married to a relative of General W. T. Sherman of the Union forces, and it is easy to speculate the expensive and ostentatious furnishings were left intact by the invaders because of that kinship. General Grant slept in the front bedroom as a guest of the house. Cedar Grove is now a commercial bed and breakfast establishment and is open for tours throughout the year.

Balfour, corner of Cherry Street and Crawford, is another antebellum home open for tours. This home takes on a particular poignancy due to its rigid adherence to restoration and preservation guidelines. The authenticity of the spartan dwelling, along with its elliptical spiral staircase, would be reason enough to visit. But this home's association with the seige has grown with time because the mistress of the house, Emma Balfour, kept a diary of those times.

Like much of Vicksburg, Balfour House was often caught in the middle as the opposing armies fired at each other's positions. As the cannon fire from the east and west passed over her home, often hitting the house and raining fragments of shell in

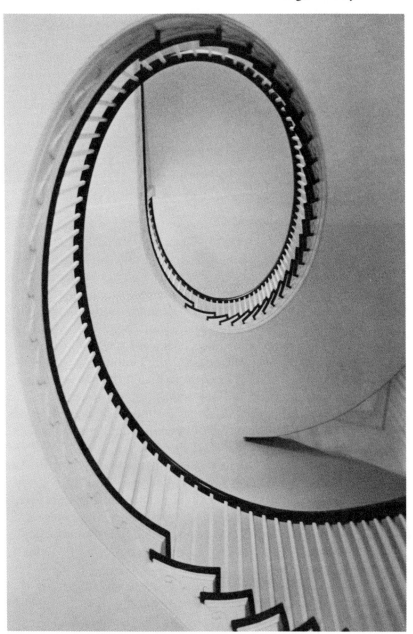

Stairwell, Balfour House, Vicksburg.

the yard, Emma Balfour wrote of the ordeal. She recorded the retreat of the Confederate army into the city, the desperate condition of the soldiers, of the citizens retreating to caves dug into the loess hills at night for a sense of safety when sleeping, of short rations and of church services in sanctuaries reduced to shambles. General J. C. Pemberton of the CSA had his headquarters one house away and the Sisters of Mercy had their convent/headquarters across the street. When the city surrendered on July 4, 1863, the Union forces set up their administrative offices in the Balfour house. Today the guides offer unembellished stories of the house's history, giving Balfour a rare dignity for a "tour" home.

Other antebellum homes in the city also have stories to entice visitors. Anchuca, Choctaw for Happy Home, 1010 First East Street, was once the home of Jefferson Davis' brother Joseph. Davis Island, where Joseph's legendary Hurricane Plantation, as well as Jefferson's more modest home and plantation were located, is near here. Today about 12 miles south of town, the island still looms in the haze. The Union forces burned Joseph's home, but not Jefferson's. Local historians speculate that since Jefferson was president of the CSA, the Union soldiers mistakenly thought the more opulent home on the island was his. What the Union forces did not destroy, time has. Jefferson's home, Brierfield, burned during the 1930s. There are no roads to the island. Boats are required to cross from the mainland. Locals say visits to the island are discouraged.

But visitors are encouraged to visit just about every other site in and around Vicksburg. The Court House Museum (Cherry Street) with its eclectic collection of memorabilia from before, during and after the Civil War, is a prime spot for people who want to not only see artifacts but stop and talk about the past. The museum director Gordon Cotton is considered by locals the expert on all matters historical.

The town is so rich with history you will probably want to stay longer than you originally planned.

Vicksburg is located on US 80 and I-20 about 40 miles west of Jackson. Accommodations are numerous, as are fast food establishments and a variety of restaurants. The town is visitor oriented and is one of the most accessible in the state for history lovers.

For free maps, brochures on area attractions and other information, contact the Vicksburg-Warren County Tourist Commission, P. O. Box 110, Vicksburg, MS 39180. Telephone 601-636-9421 in state. Out of state telephone 800-221-3536. The tourist information office is located across Clay Street from Vicksburg National Military Park.

The Spirit of Vicksburg sight-seeing excursion boat operates year-round. Dinner and moonlight dancing cruises are seasonal. Dock is at the foot of Clay Street. Address: P.O. Box 1405, Vicksburg, MS 39180. Telephone 601-634-6059. Admission fee charged.

The Vanishing Glory, a visual presentation of Vicksburg's war time story, located in the old train depot, at the corner of Grove and Levee Streets, is open daily. Shows each hour on the hour, 10 a.m. to 8 p.m. Address: 500 Grove Street, Vicksburg, MS 39180. Telephone 601-634-1863. Admission fee charged.

Old Court House Museum, Court House Square, Cherry Street, Vicksburg, MS 39180. Open Monday through Saturday, 8:30 a.m. to 4:30 p.m. and on Sunday afternoons from 1:30 p.m. to 4:30 p.m. Closed Thanksgiving, Christmas Eve, Christmas Day and New Year's Day. Admission fee charged.

Balfour House, corner of Crawford and Cherry, is open daily from 9 a.m. to 5 p.m. Address: P.O. Box 1541, Vicksburg, MS 39180. Telephone 601-638-3690. Admission fee charged.

Cedar Grove, 2200 Oak Street, Vicksburg, MS 39180. Telephone 800-862-1300 out-of-state. Telephone 601-636-1605 in Mississippi. Open daily from 9 a.m. to 5 p.m. Admission fee charged.

Anchuca, 1010 First East Street, Vicksburg, MS 39180. Telephone 800-262-4822 or 601-636-4931. Open daily from 9 a.m. to 5 p.m. Tours at other times by appointment. Admission fee charged.

13
The Delta, Greenville, and Winterville Mounds

North of Vicksburg US Highway 61 runs out of the kudzu shrouded hills, crosses the Yazoo River and streaks out into the flat land of the legendary Delta. The Delta is the land that loves cotton. The romance has been going on since antebellum days. Occasionally a flirtation with soybeans, corn or sorghum appears to be blossoming into a more meaningful relationship, but every speck of black earth whispers nothing could ever replace cotton in the Delta's heart.

A sage once proclaimed, "The Delta begins in the lobby of the Peabody (a hotel in Memphis) and ends at Catfish Row in Vicksburg." This has become the accepted standard of the regions's boundaries—at least poetically.

The Great River Road, which turns up MS 1 at Onward, offers an unparalleled journey through the heart of the Delta. The historic marker at Onward recalls that Teddy Roosevelt once went bear hunting in the vicinity and supposedly spared a baby bear's life, thus becoming the patron saint of the stuffed animals called "Teddy bears." The side of the store at Onward (there's only one) sports a colorful mural of cotton pickers, wagons, mules and fields. You won't have to travel too far on MS 1 before you'll see modern day field workers. In midsummer there are still crews of workers armed with hoes "chopping" cotton in the fields that stretch for miles either side of the road.

This is not a land of antebellum mansions. Homes along the road are mostly modest and after you've stated the land is flat, loves cotton, and stretches on to ennui, there are few other odes to be written.

South of Greenville a few homes more in keeping with the

Mississippi Welcome Station, Greenville.

antebellum stereotype appear. From MS 1 go west to US 82 via MS 454 so you won't miss the Mississippi Welcome Station. Built as a replica sternwheeler riverboat and "moored" on its own little pond, this Welcome Station is a fun photographic backdrop as well as being historically symbolic of the business and commerce in the area. A garden patch has sample rows of rice, soybeans, cotton, peanuts, sorghum and corn. Exotic lavender lilies grow on the pond. The park-like surroundings are shaded with oaks, willows, poplars, maples, pecans and china berry trees.

The town site of Greenville has been moved several times—but never any great distance from the site of the present town which was once part of Blantonia Plantation. The first town of Greenville was destroyed by floods, the second was burned by fire from Union gunboats in 1863 then caved into the river. The third town was incorporated in 1870. After losing large portions of its landmass in 1927 when the town was under water for 70 days, higher and wider levees were built. But more drastic action seemed necessary. So in 1935 the course of the Mississippi was changed to run several miles west of the city. Greenville's waterfront is now located on Lake Ferguson which joins the Mississippi south of town.

There is an annual pilgrimage of the town's southern-styled and Victorian homes. But history takes on a deeper more profound meaning than architecture and century-old memorabilia in Greenville. Here you can explore pre-history, actually peer into the times before men left records.

The Winterville Mounds three miles north of town on MS 1 are the legacy of another people whose life rhythms were also probably dictated by the river. A 40-acre state park is on the site and in 1966 a museum resembling a mound was built. On an early summer's day, a yellow crop dusting plane rises over the tree line, then swoops down, buzzing nearby fields, delivering the immature cotton a prescribed dose of some mysterious concoction to aid its growth. The ancient people, the Native American members of the Mississippian culture who built this ceremonial city and occupied it for approximately six centuries, were also farmers. They probably performed plant tending rituals that would appear as intriguing as the crop duster's.

Winterville's great central mound is now about 50 feet high. Archaeologists estimate that it was probably over 100 feet high when in use. Only 11 mounds are left within the park grounds; several are just outside the compound on private land, but there were probably from 23 to 30 in earlier times. Archaeologists and anthropologists often remind laymen that dealing with pre-history means you can't always be precise. Sometimes at best you can only make a "scientific guess." But they have pieced together enough of the Winterville Mounds' story to help us visualize that ancient place.

The flat-topped mounds with rectangular bases that are found at Winterville were usually where the elite members of society erected their homes. The chief's would be on the highest mound with the lesser nobility and priests' dwellings on the smaller ones. Temples, council houses, as well as the schools of teachers and craftsmen would also be erected on mounds. Burial mounds were usually conical. An anthropologist did

Highest mound at Winterville Mounds near Greenville.

discover over 20 skeletons in one such mound here. But most of the mounds here were non-burial sites. At its height Winterville had a population of 15,000 to 20,000 people. The people who supported the society didn't live in the city itself but in the countryside. Winterville was probably similar to the capital of a state in the Mississippian culture. Cahokia in Illinois, across the river from St. Louis, was probably the equivalent of a national Mississippian capital. Winterville's two primary plazas were the site of ceremonies and ballgames.

Though it is believed that by the time of De Soto's expedition through the area Winterville's temples were already falling into ruin, diaries of expedition members offer clues to the lifestyles of the people. The diarists described in detail the

Mississippians they encountered even to their hair style—which was long, straight and cut away from their face. In the museum here are also artifacts of De Soto's expedition. Copper bells have been identified and dated by experts as being made in the Spanish city from which the De Soto expedition set out for the New World at the appropriate time. Trade beads and an iron broadax of the period have not been so positively identified, but there is circumstantial evidence to suggest they are also from the expedition. However the museum's great treasures are the Native American pottery and the pre-Columbian artifacts on display not only from Winterville but also from other sites in the Delta. There is a skeleton of a Mississippian in a recreated burial. The Mississippians were the ancestors of the Choctaw and Chickasaw. The modern Mississippi Choctaw have given the museum samples of crafts for display.

Atop the highest mound with the hot summer sun grilling human skin, the wind rustling the tall tangle of grass, the view reminds visitors of just how close to immortality the Delta ventures.

Greenville is located on MS 1 and US 82. Winterville Mounds Park is located three miles north of Greenville on MS 1. The Winterville Mounds Park with picnic grounds, restrooms and 40 acres of mounds is free to the public. The museum on the grounds does charge an admission fee.

For the Great River Road tour through this portion of the Delta, take US 61 north of Vicksburg to the intersection of MS 1 at Onward. Greenville's Welcome Station with information, picnic facilities and restrooms is west of town on US 82 from the River Road (MS 1) take MS 545 to US 82. Stay on US 82 East after leaving the Welcome Station. This highway junctions with MS 1 in town. Accommodations, fast food establishments and restaurants are located in Greenville.

For information about the area, contact the Washington County Welcome Center, Highway 82 at Reed Road, P. O. Box 6022, Greenville, MS 38704. Telephone 601-332-2378.

14
Clarksdale

Out in the middle of the intersection, where US 49 crosses US 61, Robert Johnson dickered with the devil. Folks say he sold his soul for the ability to play the blues better than any other man. The same folks go on to say if you had ever heard him play, you wouldn't doubt it for a minute. This is how the history of the blues goes. Reality and fantasy may be one and the same. They bear no identifying marks.

Sid Graves has corraled large chunks of the blues, memorabilia, myths, legends and even scholarly books in the Delta Blues Museum and housed it in the old Carnegie Public Library here in Clarksdale. You can spend hours listening to tapes and records, or watching video recordings of a wide cross section of the blues greats. Their names are like a litany for the faithful. Eddie "Son" House, John Lee Hooker, Howlin' Wolf, Muddy Waters, B.B. King. There are photos and a jukebox, guitars and a harmonica. Most of all there is Sid Graves' boundless enthusiasm for the museum and the blues. He serves as an interpreter for the non-Delta soul seeking enlightenment.

Highway 61 is legendary in the lyrics and the lives of the blues musicians. Graves says, "It takes them in and it takes them out," simplifying the comings and goings from the music's heartland. Bessie Smith, perhaps the most famous female blues singer ever, died here after a car wreck on US 61 in 1937. But it was the birth of so many practitioneers of this illusive art form in the immediate vicinity of Clarksdale that makes the area unique. However, Graves says if W. C. Handy hadn't moved here back in 1903, the blues may have never got off the ground, much less out of the cotton fields and juke joints. Handy became interested in the local black "folk" music when he saw

Blues musician Wade Walton opens the door to the world of the latest Delta Blues for visitors to his barbership near the Delta Blues Museum, Clarksdale.

how much money was showered on practitioneers by audiences at impromptu performances. He is credited with being the first to arrange and score traditional blues as a framework for larger compositions.

Thousands of visitors from all over the world come to this blues shrine every year. They are not usually casual tourists, but people looking for the history, the roots of American music. The exotic world of the Delta is an added dividend. After a stint in the museum Graves recommends they look up Wade Walton at Walton's Blues Barbershop, 304 Fourth Street. Walton always knows who's playing where locally. He's a musician himself and between customers might be prevailed upon to perform.

The soul searching of the blues, the rhythm of the music and the language inspired more than musicians. Tennessee Williams spent much of his boyhood here with his grandfather at the red brick St. George's Episcopal Church and the modest rectory next door at 106 Sharkey Street. In the rich, rounded tones of the Delta, Williams recorded his poem "I'm a gold tooth woman with the gold tooth blues." His play *Cat on a Hot Tin Roof* captures the essence of life in the Delta. Another Mississippi literary giant, William Faulkner, also used the area as a setting for the short story *The Bear*.

A potpourri of historic fact emerges. (Nathan Bedford Forrest joined the Confederate army here.) But Clarksdale's Native American past overshadows all else. In pre-Columbian times this spot on the Sunflower River was a community of some 3000 souls. Two important Indian trading routes crossed here, the Chakchiuma Trail which ran northeast to Pontotoc, and the Lower Creek Trail which ran from the Georgia coast to the southern California coast. The Indians called their fortified town Quiz-Quiz. De Soto's expedition visited here in 1541. Locals joke, "De Soto was our first tourist." Old records state the band of adventurers took the town ". . . by assault and captured much people and clothes. . . ." Then in a completely uncharacteristic gesture, De Soto, fearful of an uprising, "returned to the Indians what was theirs. . . ." A few days later, historians believe, men of De Soto's expedition saw the Mis-

sissippi for the first time. The vicinity of Friar's Point is given as
the location of De Soto's first sighting of the "great river." The
Carnegie Public Library (next door to and adjoining the Delta
Blues Museum) houses an extensive collection of relics of Quiz-
Quiz and the surrounding pre-Columbian Native American
communities in Coahoma (Choctaw for Red Panther) County.

Modern day Clarksdale may be one of those fabled "livable"
small towns where people partake of a near idyllic lifestyle—a
place where boys on bicycles sling sacks of the *Clarksdale
Register* over their shoulders each afternoon and ride down oak-
canopied streets tossing the evening edition onto lawns of
veranda encased homes. Should boredom set in, the world of
the blues lyric composers and the emotions that inspired
Tennessee Williams are only as far away as anyone wants them
to be.

Clarksdale is located at the intersection of US 49 and US 61
about 150 miles northwest of Jackson. Accommodations are
available in town, also a wide variety of ethnic restaurants.
Address for The Delta Blues Museum and Carnegie Library is
114 Delta Street, P.O. Box 280, Clarksdale, MS 38614. Telephone 601-624-4461. Hours 9 a.m. until 5 p.m. Monday
through Friday. Admission free.

15
Florewood River Plantation

The smell of the damp humus, the aroma of black earth being turned by plows, floats across the cypress swamp, filters through the fragile new-green leaves of the sweet gum and tupelo trees to greet visitors at Florewood River Plantation as the first warm breezes of spring dance along the banks of the Yazoo in Mississippi cotton country.

Visions of long ago come to life as red mules pull steel plows through the black soil, and men in slouch hats, woolen pants and homemade brogans sow the seeds of summer's harvest.

Come autumn the same men and mules will be supplying the man and horsepower to operate a sorghum mill and cook the juice into thick brown molasses.

Early December will find the plantation slipping into a Christmas dress of red ribbons, cedar wreaths and glossy magnolia leaves. Handmade candles will light the planter's house as well as the outbuildings in the re-enactment of an antebellum Christmas celebration. Apples and cornshuck dolls are sample gifts for children in the slave quarters. Costumed carolers looking like transplants from a Charles Dickens novel sing the ancient hymns of the season. Spicy molasses cookies and warm cider are served to all guests.

This is "living history" on a replica cotton plantation which is also a Mississippi State Park. Costumed interpreters act out the everyday activities of an antebellum-frontier homestead with the cycle of seasonal activities giving the actor-interpreters a never-ending drama to portray.

In the kitchen behind the big house where the fruits of the harvest are cooked, all visitors are offered a taste of the dish of the day. Sometimes it is cornbread, greens, peas or stew. Other times hot biscuits sopped with molasses are the offered treats. All dishes are cooked in the kitchen's fireplace or on the hearth in a three-legged dutch oven with hot coals heaped on top. The cook, in a long sweeping gown and colorful turban, tells stories of antebellum plantation life on the Mississippi frontier as she dishes out the stew. Stretching up to her full height she proclaims, "The cook was the most important person on the plantation." The interpreter in this living history demonstration has developed a multi-dimension personality for her character. The other interpreters in this plantation drama are just as believable in their portrayals.

An elderly southern belle greets visitors at the front door of the big house. Wearing a cotton day-dress made from a period pattern, the belle makes an appearance as delicate as magnolia fragrance on a spring breeze. Upstairs she points out Confederate General Nathan Bedford Forrest's half-tester rosewood bed and wig-dresser. She speaks of by-gone customs, "Little boys slept in the rooms with their parents until they were six or seven years old, then they were sent to an out-building on the place. Girls stayed in the house until they were married."

In a second upstairs bedroom she points out a small corner table set for tea. "Children took tea in their own room. They were not allowed in the parlor," she explains. A set of novels by Sir Walter Scott and sparse writing implements are on a desk. The ancient belle softly asks if there are any questions before leading her guests back down the stairs.

Across the back yard the walkway leads to a delicate white trellis where red roses cling, hiding a necessity of antebellum life, the privy. Wash houses with wells, wooden tubs and raised ribbed rub boards that must have kept many a laundress's knuckles raw; hoppers where ashes were collected for making lye soap; smoke houses for preserving meats; servants' quarters and a carriage house with a room for the tutor at the end; the loom room and sewing house; the barns and wagon sheds; the infirmary; the overseer's house—26 buildings in all make up the complex. But it is the special touches added by the costumed interpreters that bring the place to life: the overseer's wife fussing about her chores, the blacksmith sweating over his

Wagon, Florewood River Plantation near Greenwood.

Horses and mules earn their keep at Florewood River Plantation.

forge; the candlemaker's endless job of providing light for the big house, and the potter's skillful hands caressing wet lumps of clay into necessary utensils.

The frontier antebellum cotton plantation was a complete community unto itself. Though a fondness for imported goods might be displayed in the furnishings of the owners, there was no dependency on the world beyond the plantation for the necessities. Self-sufficiency was the order of the day for all the basics including religion and education.

A church on the place did double duty as a school house. An interpreter-tutor stands in the doorway waiting to share the antebellum educational experience with visitors.

Clearing up misconceptions of plantation life is not necessarily a mission of the state park, neither is glorifying an era of questionable moral and social practices. A spokesman for the park says, "We simply offer an objective, historic view. This is how it was."

With the musky smell of upturned earth scenting the spring air, it is easy to believe life was good in the cotton plantation world of long ago. But in late summer, with the sun broiling the dusty, black meadows, walking among the tall cotton stalks, stooping along the rows to reach a choice ball, scratched by briars and stung by nettles that have escaped the chopper's hoes, visitors may develop another opinion.

Florewood River Plantation is two miles west of Greenwood on US 82. Hours 9 a.m. to 5 p.m. Tuesday through Saturday and 1 p.m. to 5 p.m. on Sundays. A museum at the park is free. There is an admission charge for the plantation grounds and tour. For more information write Florewood River Plantation, Box 680, Greenwood, MS 38930. Telephone 601-455-3821.

Accommodations, fast food establishments and restaurants are located in Greenwood.

16
Greenwood

"There's always a job in the cotton business if you can change with the times," Pershing Chassaniol says. He's a cotton factor with offices on the banks of the Yazoo a couple of blocks away from the Leflore County Courthouse in Greenwood. Operating the business his father started when he came up from New Orleans in 1912, Chassaniol's offices are a virtual museum.

A bright, freshly painted five-cent Coca Cola sign out front marks his business, Chassaniol and Robertson, Cotton Factors. He commissioned the mural himself as an artful reminder of by-gone days, not as an advertisement. The tall desks, stools, tables and even the safe in the office where he regularly conducts business are now antiques. His father brought the business furnishings here from New Orleans. That gentleman worked for a firm in Liverpool, England, and moved to Greenwood in the wake of the great expansion of the cotton kingdom that eventually catapulted Greenwood into its self-proclaimed position as "Cotton Capital of the World." This growth was a direct result of the federal levee system that opened up hundreds of thousands of acres of swampland for cotton production. In antebellum days Greenwood did ship cotton, but in the early 20th century, thanks to the levees, Greenwood was marketing cotton. In 1928 the Cotton Exchange was incorporated and today is one of nine spot cotton markets in the nation and one of the five top world markets.

Chassanoil's business is now computerized. Worn antique chairs are clustered in a careless circle around video display terminals where the latest market news flashes across the screen in series of numbers only the initiated understand. Several tables are placed under banks of florescent lights. "We can class cotton 24 hours a day now. Before it had to be classed under true north light. Couldn't class on cloudy days." In the main room, under the skylights, Chassanoil pulls a sample from a bale and demonstrates the ancient method of classing cotton. He pulls a wad back and forth, in the same manner as taffy is pulled. "You break the cotton to see how long the fiber is," he says.

"In the fall mill men from the east would come to buy the cotton. Now we have buyers from Taiwan and Japan. Everywhere. But the cotton farmer always says, you don't have your cotton crop until you've picked it and it's in the compress. There are quite a few gins here . . . the cotton is ginned, put into 500-pound bales and then goes to the compress."

On the long lazy days between February and late August when the business is running slow, Chassanoil welcomes visitors who want to stop and chat. Just follow Front Street down the river bank from the courthouse for two blocks and look for the five-cent Coca Cola sign.

The chimes on the courthouse clock, pitched to the tones of Westminister's chimes in London, add an unexpected somber

Leaves of cotton plant growing on the grounds of Cottonlandia Museum, Greenwood.

note to the clammer of traffic around the square. According to legend Choctaw Indians used the courthouse site for ceremonial rituals of trial and execution. Greenwood's riverfront homes west of the courthouse on River Road and those north of the courthouse, across the river via Courthouse Bridge, speak eloquently of the town's lifestyles—lifestyles cotton built.

Greenwood's mind is never far from cotton, culturally or economically. The local museum is called Cottonlandia, and is located on the Highway 49-82 Bypass West. (River Road from the courthouse runs back to the Bypass; cross the river there and follow the signs to Cottonlandia.)

Cottonlandia tells the story of this land, the Delta, the people who have lived here and their relationship with the land. The land has yielded a 450-million-year-old Brachiopod, a fossil that is "the oldest thing in the museum." Wooly mammoths, masatodons, and ancient whales are among the fossilized creatures from the area that are represented in the collection. Many artifacts found in and around Greenwood are of the Mississippian culture of Native America. Sophisticated pottery symbolic of religious effigies, human and animal, are displayed along with more pragmatic pieces. Types of the first ceramics in North America, clay cooking balls from the Poverty Point Culture, along with the sophisticated beadwork of more modern Native Americans, form another part of the museum's mosiac of natural history. The museum takes pride in an extensive collection of trade beads from around the world. Farm implements used in the area over the centuries are displayed.

Artifacts from the home of the Choctaw chief, wealthy businessman, planter, state legislator for whom the town and county were named—Greenwood Leflore—are also on display. Leflore's home Malmaison was located about 12 miles northeast of town. Today a two-mile-long Nature Trail leads through a tangled jungle on the Malmaison Game Refuge surrounding the old home site. The mansion with its opulent French furnishings burned many years ago. Long before then, the man, who as chief of the western district of the Choctaw nation was one of the Choctaw's three presiding chiefs signing the Treaty of Dancing Rabbit Creek in which the majority of the Choctaw nation agreed to remove to Oklahoma, was repudiated by the Choctaw. After the treaty, as a wealthy planter winning election to the Mississippi state legislature, he again earned the wrath of people he represented by refusing to side with the Confederacy. He chose to retain his American citizenship and throughout the Civil War flew the stars and stripes from Malmaison. His grave on the Malmaison grounds has been robbed, and according to William Hony, director of Cottonlandia, the calumet (peace pipe) buried with him has surfaced in a private collection.

An unexpected treat at Cottonlandia is Miss Perle's Native Garden just outside the front door. Yucca plants, yellow-faced daisies, palmetto, columbine, ebony spleenwort fern, lamb's ear, honeysuckle, calla lilies, rain lilies, Stokes aster, sundrop, blue-eyed grass, wild white indigo—the list goes on and on—remind visitors of the rich variety of native plant life.

Cottonlandia is located on the Highway 49-82 Bypass West in Greenwood. Address: P.O. Box 1635, Greenwood, MS 38930. Telephone 601-453-0925. Admission fee charged.

Leflore County Courthouse is at the corner of Front Street and Fulton.

Chassanoil and Robertson, Cotton Factors, is two blocks east of the courthouse by the five-cent Coca Cola sign. Admission free.

Malmaison Nature Trail is about 12 miles northeast of town. Take MS 13 towards Grenada. A sign marks the trail. Admission free.

Accommodations, fast food establishments and restaurants are plentiful in town.

17
Oxford

Early 19th century Mississippians favored frontiers, the ragged edges of the known world along which timid souls did not venture. The frontier attitude spilled over into all their endeavors—even education. The University of Mississippi, "Ole Miss," established here in 1844, departed from the well-worn paths of traditional higher education to pioneer new approaches. Most universities of the period were emphasizing Greek, Latin and the classics. The new school focused on science and scientific methods.

The equipment used to demonstrate theories and scientific principles at the university before the Civil War are on display at the Kate Skipworth Museum. The museum on the edge of the campus at the foot of University Avenue has these heirlooms mainly because for so many years after the war the school (and state) was too poor to replace them with more modern equipment.

Ole Miss's pioneering professors did not neglect Greek, Latin or the classics. Their interests in ancient cultures inspired their students to revere the past—the world of the Greeks and Romans—as they prepared for the future. The popular culture of the antebellum South was infatuated with Sir Walter Scott's romantic novels based on British history and legend. Young men at the university often staged "tilting" tournaments full of pageantry and fantasy that they patterned after the jousts of that writer's romances. Sir Walter Scott's works eventually slipped into the realm of passing fads, but the deep abiding reverence for the ancient worlds of Greece and Rome didn't.

The Kate Skipworth Museum is a repository of what director Lucy Turnbull calls "the best" collection of Greco-Roman antiquities in the South. Though most pieces in the collection were a bequest of a professor who came to the university in 1949, they are symbolic of the school's long standing interests.

The "vision" paintings of Theora Hamblett (1895–1977) are also housed in the museum's collections. These naive works offer an uninhibited view of the southern soul in folk terms. They document the history of one woman's inner world. A schoolteacher who turned her home into a boarding house for college students, Theora Hamblett grew up on a farm and never ventured far in her lifestyle from the pragmatic values such an upbringing instills. But her spirit knew no boundaries. Her work was much in demand and in her later years she was represented by a New York art gallery. Her sprawling, but modest, Oxford home (circa 1872) is located on Van Buren Avenue.

The late novelist and author of Mississippiana, Stark Young's house is situated between the university campus and the Skipworth Museum. The Barnard Observatory on campus is another symbol of the high aspirations the pre-Civil War university had. Built to house one of the most advanced and powerful telescopes of the period, the war prevented its delivery. The Observatory is now the home of the Center for the Study of Southern Culture. Films on southern subjects—from folklife, folk artists, blues musicians to William Faulkner and his works—are available for viewing by visitors.

The university owns many of the most notable historic attractions in town. After the Battle of Shiloh (April 1862), the buildings on the campus were used as a hospital for the wounded. U. S. Grant and his Union troops occupied the town for much of December 1862. In late August, 1864, Union forces burned the town. Legends persist that Union troops rode their horses through the university's most hallowed halls in one of their milder insult modes.

Today Oxford, Mississippi, could be a fictional town, a place sprung from the old black manual typewriter of William Faulkner. But the Nobel Prize winner didn't invent Oxford—he just captured its likeness, painted it in words, put a thin wash of fiction over a real life mask. If you come here looking for his

Mississippi novelist William Faulkner's home, Rowan Oak, in evening shadows, Oxford.

Faulkner's typewriter on display at Rowan Oak, Oxford.

fictional Jefferson, Yoknapatawpha County, you won't be disappointed.

The people and memories lurking behind the white-columned mansions' doors and peering from the far side of lace curtains at the windows of rainbow-hued gingerbread cottages are familiar. They bear striking resemblances to the fabled storekeepers, school teachers, sewing machine salesmen, bankrupt planters, iron-willed matriarchs, their sons and daughters, ancient maiden aunts, lawyers and business men who-hunt-in-the-fall as well as the dreamers and even the notorious Count No-count.

As a child Faulkner (1897–1962) lived at the corner of South 11th and Buchanan Streets. A broad meadow, a unique feature in the compact neighborhood, stretches back to a Gothic Victorian cottage surrounded by flowers and bushy trees. A few blocks away, on South Lamar, Faulkner visited his grandparents in their massive white Colonial Revival house. He lived at the Victorian hilltop Duvall House on University Avenue when he wrote his most famous short story, *A Rose for Miss Emily* and the steamy novel *Sanctuary*. This was the home to which he brought his bride, "Miss Estelle," in 1929 after their marriage at the Cottage Hill Presbyterian Church. Built in 1840 the church is the oldest in the county and rich in the texture and feel of age with its gated pews, plastered walls, and outside, with its tall cedars and massive magnolias sheltering the church yard cemetery. Across town, out MS 30, a gravel road leads to the farm, Greenfields, where Faulkner and his brother raised mules.

But it is Faulkner's home, Rowan Oak, at the bend in Old Taylor Road, that is most associated with the creation of his masterpieces. He moved into the antebellum house, circa 1842, in 1930 and lived there until his death in 1962. The master's studio, his writing room, is an annex to the library. Furnished with wooden lawn chairs, a narrow cot, a crude home-made desk, an antique manual typewriter, a clutter of empty ink bottles and tobacco tins, the writing room contains one of Faulkner's most dynamic works. *A Fable,* a novel, is here a mural. The artist outlined the work on the walls of his studio.

The house is owned by the University of Mississippi, where Faulkner himself was once a student. However he lacked the patience for classroom learning and left after less than a year. He did take on odd jobs at the university—such as painting the outside woodwork of Ventress Hall, a red brick turreted fortress that was once the school's library. His most notable position on campus was as postmaster. Legend has it that he was the worst postmaster in the history of the school. After a couple of years he quit because as he allegedly put it, "I don't care to be at the beck and call of any fool who can afford a two-cent stamp."

The university's J.D. Williams Library proudly displays Faulkner's Nobel Prize (1950), a legion of other awards and honors, first edition prints of his books, early hand written manuscripts and posters from the movies made from his work. *Intruder in the Dust* was filmed here in 1949 and debuted at the Lyric Theatre, now One Health Center, just off the courthouse square.

The town was also the setting for another movie, *Home from the Hills.* Fiddler's Folly, a prefab Victorian mansion that was shipped in during the 1880s, was the heroine's home in the film. Star William Holden's hero resided at Ammadelle, a proud red brick antebellum mansion. The houses are neighbors on North Lamar Street.

The best entertainment in the 150-year-old town beyond the university's attractions is the town itself. It is as hypnotic as a good book. Stake out a bench on the courthouse square and you'll be in the center of all Oxford's activities—real and imagined.

Oxford is located 20 miles east of I-55 on MS 6 about 165 miles northeast of Jackson and about 48 miles west of Tupelo.

Rowan Oak, Old Taylor Road, is open Monday through Friday 10 a.m. to Noon and 2 p.m. to 4 p.m. Saturday 10 a.m. to Noon. Sunday 2 p.m. to 4 p.m. Telephone 601-234-3284. Admission free.

J. D. Williams Library and The Center for the Study of Southern Culture, on the university campus, as well as the Kate Skipworth Museum, on University Avenue, just off campus, vary their hours due to school activities and schedules. Call the office of University Relations 601-232-7318 for updated schedules. Admission free.

For a free detailed map of Oxford with all area attractions marked and other information, contact the Oxford-Lafayette County Chamber of Commerce, 440 North Lamar, P.O. Box 147, Oxford, Mississippi 38655. Telephone 601-234-4651.

Accommodations, fast food establishments and restaurants are plentiful in town.

18
Holly Springs

Holly Springs' annual pilgrimage of antebellum homes is the envy of towns for miles around. Genteel ladies in other regional municipalities speak in the steely-soft accent of the agrieved, "What do you expect? Those women up there just did everything in the world they could think of to keep those Yankee soldiers entertained, to keep their minds off burning the town." Then in the smug tone of the self-righteous they add, "Our town was burned."

Though historic gossip is more entertaining than malicious, especially when the events under examination occurred well over a hundred years ago, Bea Green, a resident of Holly Springs, says there is more than a little truth to the allegations. A storyteller of uncommon ability, she says, "One of the reasons Holly Springs was not burned to the ground was because the local ladies were so charming."

It seems that during "The War," as the Civil War is most commonly called in these parts, a certain group of local women did turn their attention to keeping the Union troops entertained. Though, exactly what these females' purpose was is questionable. The names of the women who were friendly with the northern soldiers are remembered, passed on from generation to generation. It might be some comfort for the ladies of neighboring towns to know that long time residents of Holly Springs do not speak of these fraternizers in endearing terms. One of the more elegant homes on the pilgrimage tours, the Greek Revival mansion, Wakefield, circa 1858, was once the home of one of the women who scandalized the town. After the war she went so far as to marry a Union officer.

The war overshadows all else here. General U. S. Grant set up headquarters for his Federal forces in Holly Springs and at one point brought his family down and quartered them in a local mansion.

There are 13 Confederate generals buried in Hillcrest Cemetery, and during the war the town changed hands between Confederate and Union troops so many times local historians have lost count. By one account the town suffered 61 raids, the most dramatic of which was lead by the Confederate general, Earl Van Dorn. In 1862 when Grant was planning his attack on Vicksburg he moved his base of supplies from Memphis to Holly Springs. When Grant left town for a meeting with other Union commanders before their planned move on Vicksburg, Van Dorn's rebel raiders, about 3,500 Confederate cavalrymen, attacked the town unexpectedly destroying and/or confiscating Grant's winter stores. Some historians believe Van Dorn's raid delayed the success of Grant's operations against Vicksburg. (In the spirit of gossiping fairness, it should be noted that in 1863, General Van Dorn was assassinated in Spring Hill, Tennessee, by a prominent doctor who claimed the general had been "involved" with his wife. The general was from Port Gibson and is buried there.)

Before the war, before there was a town named Holly Springs, the area was in the Chickasaw nation. According to legends the area was at the crossroads of Indian trails where travelers stopped to rest and bathe in the medicinal springs which were in a glade surrounded by holly trees. The town was founded in 1837, five years after the Chickasaw Cession.

The Holly Springs Garden Club members are fond of reminding visitors that their town has been preserved rather than restored. The entire Courthouse Square is on the National Register of Historic Places. Two antebellum churches, Christ Episcopal, circa 1858, and First United Methodist, circa 1839, offer an idea of the intensity of antebellum church services in their architecture and furnishings. The Marshall County Historical Museum's home is the former Mississippi Synodical College, College Avenue, two blocks east of the Square. The museum contains artifacts and memorabilia from area residents.

The pilgrimage in April each year is a good time to visit

Montrose, Holly Springs.

Holly Springs. Then visitors are offered an opportunity to explore the town's wide variety of architecture ranging across the economic spectrum from mansion to modest cottage. Some of the noteworthy examples are: Airliewood, circa 1858, Gothic Revival; Cedarhurst, circa 1857, French Gothic and Dunvegan, circa 1845, an early Holly Springs cottage. Montrose, circa 1858, the home of the Holly Springs Garden Club, is open year round by appointment. Of particular interest inside Montrose is the circular stairway; outside, Montrose's grounds are graced with an arboretum which contains 37 different specimens of trees native to the area, each specimen is labeled with its common and botanical name.

Phillips' Grocery is also open for business year round—the "in" spot in modern-day Holly Springs, located on Van Dorn Avenue across the road from the red brick Gothic train depot. A hamburger at the grocery, which is a real grocery, on Saturdays is a tradition among townspeople. The grocery was a saloon in Reconstruction times. Some of the best stories in town are dished out at the grocery, but few top Bea Green's version of a local favorite. It seems a certain proper Victorian lady, named Mrs. Smith, was in the habit of going for lengthy carriage rides. One day when she returned early and unexpectedly from a ride, she found her husband, also a very proper Victorian, in a compromising position with the family maid. Undaunted the gentleman looked his wife straight in the eyes and said, "Mrs. Smith, I fear I've lost my mind."

Holly Springs is located on US 78 in north central Mississippi about 60 miles northwest of Tupelo and 30 miles north of Oxford. Some accommodations are available in town, more extensive accommodations can be found at Oxford a short drive away via MS 7.

For a map (fee charged) with antebellum sites marked, write the Holly Springs Chamber of Commerce, Box 12, Holly Springs, MS 38635. Telephone 601-252-2943.

For information about the Holly Springs Pilgrimage or Montrose, write: Holly Springs Garden Club, Inc., P. O. Box 696, Holly Springs, MS 38635.

Marshall County Museum, College Ave, two blocks east of the courthouse square, open Monday, Tuesday, Wednesday and Friday 9 a.m. to 11 a.m. and 2 p.m. to 4 p.m. Thursdays 9 a.m. to 11 a.m. Closed Thursday afternoons, weekends and legal holidays. Admission fee charged.

19
Corinth and Northeast Mississippi

The message from Corinth to Richmond was prophetic. "Can we not be reinforced? . . . If defeated here we lose the Mississippi Valley and probably our cause. . . ," General P.G.T. Beauregard, CSA, warned his high command.

In April 1862 Beauregard had retreated to Corinth from Shiloh, about 20 miles away in Tennessee. He had assumed the command of the Confederate forces at Shiloh when Albert Sydney Johnston died in battle. At first the battle at Shiloh seemed to be going in the Confederates' favor. Johnston had taken the initiative. U. S. Grant and his 47,000 man Army of the Tennessee were camping near the Pittsburg Landing on the Tennessee River, awaiting the arrival of the Army of the Ohio before their planned attack on Corinth, an important prize because it was at the junction of two major railroads. The Confederates had poured their "very best" into Corinth to protect the railroads. (Even a CSA division protecting New Orleans was sent to Corinth, leaving defenses gravely weakened and perhaps hastening that city's fall to Union forces.)

Johnston marched 44,000 Confederates up from Corinth in a surprise move and caught the Union forces unawares. The battle began the morning of April 6th. At first it appeared Johnston's plan to crush the Union army on the banks of the Tennessee River would be successful, but by mid-afternoon, he fell in battle. That evening Beauregard called off the attack. When the battle resumed in the morning, the Confederates at first still appeared to be advancing. But the Union's Army of the Ohio—17,000 men strong—had arrived in the night. In the early afternoon of the second day, Beauregard began the retreat to Corinth.

The Confederates stepped up the construction of fortified breastworks in the town while townspeople were busy trying to cope with the needs of the wounded. (Southern casualties at Shiloh numbered 10,699 while northern casualties were listed at 13,047.) More Confederate troops arrived in Corinth and swelled the ranks, at least on paper, to 112,092.

More Union troops were also arriving at Pittsburg Landing; they soon numbered 128,315. In May, Union forces commander W. H. Halleck telegraphed the Secretary of War in Washington, "Richmond and Corinth are now the great strategical points of war, and our success at these points should be insured at all hazards."

According to a local historian, Halleck started his march to Corinth with a shovel, erecting earthworks "every step of the way" for almost 20 miles. Beauregard surprised everybody, especially Jefferson Davis, by retreating without even attempting a defense. (After an investigation Beauregard was relieved of his command.) On May 30 Union forces seized the town. Union officials dispersed their army throughout the immediate tri-state area. Halleck was called to Washington as a hero. The Battle of Corinth was still to come.

William Rosecrans was in charge at Corinth when his old West Point classmate, Confederate Generl Earl Van Dorn and his forces attacked on October 3rd. The Confederates seemed to be making headway but called off the attack as darkness fell. The next day they failed to break through the far right Union flank in the vicinity of the present day high school. An effort at Fort Robinett was even less successful. But the southerners were successful on the northwest side of town and poured down Jackson, Polk and Fillmore Streets. They captured Rosecrans' headquarters. Hand to hand combat erupted as the fighting engulfed most of the downtown area. By noon the tide had turned and the Confederates were driven out of town. Van Dorn withdrew to Ripley.

This is the basic information needed for a visit to Corinth. History is synonymous with the Civil War here. Actually it may be impossible to have a conversation that does not embrace the

James Franks northeast Mississippi storyteller and founder of the Franks Museum.

topic at some point. Though a local matriarch says, "We aren't as bad about the war as we used to be."

The railroads that brought Corinth such grief during the war actually gave it viability in 1855. At first called Cross City the citizens decided the name of Corinth, in honor of the Grecian city, was more in keeping with the image they wished to project.

Fort Robinett, now a small park, is the most accessible of the Civil War sites in town. Now a museum the Curlee House, circa 1857, served as quarters for Confederate General Braxton Bragg and Union General H. W. Halleck—but not at the same time. Earthworks, a rifle pit, and the federal battery sites are scattered all through the town. Some are marked. The Corinth National Cemetery, at the head of Johns' Street is the final resting place of more than 6,000 Union soldiers from 15 states. Confederate burial trenches are located in an area south of Droke Road and east of Parkway.

For a change of pace, a little "R&R"—rest and recreation— from the war zone, take US 45 south of town, then nine miles east on MS 356 to the Jacinto Courthouse, located in what was the county seat of Old Tishimingo County. Built in 1854, this proud old building deserves to be seen for its Williamsburg-styled architecture as well as the museum it houses. The town Jacinto has long since disappeared. When the county was divided into Alcorn, Prentiss and Tishomingo counties in 1870, the courthouse became a school, then in 1908 a Methodist church. It has been restored by the Jacinto Foundation which maintains a country store, a park, recreation area with nature trails, mineral springs and a swinging bridge adjoining the site.

Another interesting site near Corinth, south of Booneville, just north of Gunntown on US 45, is a homespun museum. James Franks, an elderly bearded fellow who has honed his folksy stories to a fine edge, runs an establishment he calls the Franks Museum. On display is a unique collection of one or two of every item that made life possible on a north Mississippi farm in earlier, simpler times. As a hobby Mr. Franks, as he is universally known, builds and revamps cars, many of which have been used by Hollywood movie makers to authenticate movie scenes. Mr. Franks, himself, has appeared in a movie or two and has the anecdotes to prove it. He's got a story for just about any topic you want to name. His blend of legends, folk fact and fiction as well as the history of the area is tantalizing.

Corinth is located at the junction of US 45 and US 72 in northeast Mississippi near the Tennessee border. Accommodations, restaurants and fast food establishments are located in town. Request more information from the Corinth-Alcorn Area Chamber of Commerce, P. O. Box 1049, Corinth, MS 38834. Telephone 601-287-5269.

The Curlee House, 301 Childs St., Corinth, MS 38834. Telephone 601-287-2231. Open year round, except January. Hours Monday through Sunday 1 p.m. to 4 p.m. Closed Thursdays. Other times by appointment. Admission fee charged.

Jacinto Courthouse and Village, Box 1048, Corinth, MS 38834. Telephone 601-287-7679. Located on MS 356, east of US 45 nine miles. Open April through December. Hours Tuesday through Sunday 1 p.m. to 5 p.m. or by appointment. Admission free.

Franks Museum, Highway 45 south of Booneville near Gunntown. Admission fee charged.

20
Tupelo—Elvis Presley's Birthplace

Elvis Presley's hometown is still in awe of the special place their most famous son earned in the world of music and the hearts of his fans. January 8, 1935, the "King of Rock and Roll" was born here, an event that has put this Mississippi town on the pilgrimage-styled tours thousands of people from around the world make every year.

Elvis was a good boy. Most anybody you'll meet here will tell you that, though they probably didn't know him personally during the time he lived here.

Hardly anybody living here now remembers him from those boyhood years. He moved on early. By the time he was 13 he was living in Memphis. But that didn't stop the King of Rock and Roll from becoming his hometown's favorite hero, which was probably the most difficult and personally impressive accomplishment of his lifetime.

Elvis Presley lived on the wrong side of town here. Worse than that, he was born on the wrong side of town. After he became a star, making gobs of money in the mid-'50s, he moved to the right side of town up in Memphis. Maybe not everyone understands how heart-wrenching and destructive to the soul journeys across the economic and class lines of small southern towns can be. Visiting Elvis' birthplace in Tupelo and understanding his origins may answer some of the more puzzling questions about the fabled entertainer's personality.

Vernon Presley, Elvis' daddy, borrowed $180 and built a two room, shotgun house next door to his parents in 1934. He created a tiny, spartan home for himself and his wife Gladys, a place of their own where they could shelter their love and dreams, a place where their baby Elvis could be born. About three years later the Presleys' were evicted. They couldn't scrape together the money to repay Vernon's loan. Even though they lost their home, they continued to live in Tupelo for ten more years.

When Elvis hit the big time, he came back to Tupelo and gave a benefit performance to raise money for a park, a real uptown recreational facility with a gym, swimming pool, ball courts and playing fields. There was only one stipulation, that it be built on the wrong side of town for economically and socially disadvantaged youngsters who Elvis felt would never have a chance to use such a facility otherwise.

A spokesperson for the Elvis Presley Birthplace says there were no concrete plans for Elvis' first home when the 15-acre property around the birthplace was purchased and the park opened in the late '50s. The two-room house set vacant for several years until a local garden club asked to open it as a project. The simple house, restored and refurbished to what it would have been like when Elvis lived there is now the number one attraction travelers to Elvis' hometown seek. Tourists come from all over the world, about 23,000 of them yearly, making the turn off U.S. 78 East down Elvis Presley Boulevard, to do homage at the little white house at the end of the road.

In tiny rooms, amid the simple unadorned furnishings, it is not too farfetched to guess the fans, on a true pilgrimage, commune with the departed Mississippian's spirit. They have usually visited Graceland, a hundred miles away in Memphis, before they come to Tupelo. Perhaps they ask themselves, could the child born here, wrapped in his mother's love, bounced on his daddy's knee, grow up and become the King of Rock and Roll? Could he really, one day, move into a physician's mansion in Memphis? Could anyone nurtured in the clean, simplicity of this tiny cottage aspire to the gaudy, bizarre world of Elvis' Graceland?

Guides at the birthplace say they have seen truck drivers stand in the front room and cry. No wonder. Here are the roots of ambition, Vernon's first dreams of a better life for his son. And here is the ghostly echo of Elvis' first music, his mother's lullabyes. This is the place the personality began. The Bible, the

Elvis Presley's birthplace, Tupelo.

kerosene lamp, the linoleum's flowered pattern, the family's photograph on the mantle, the thin, white chenille spread on the bed set the emotional stage. Even non-fans can feel the fleeting presence of the little family's spirit.

There's a chapel here in the park. Fans built it as a memorial. A popular site for local weddings, the chapel has no regularly scheduled religious services and is intended for private meditations. Elvis' personal Bible is on display, as is the pulpit from his boyhood church.

For the fans who want to take home some Elvis memento, there is a souvenir shop in the lobby of the park's gym, also called the Visitors' Center. Tourists buy everything from post cards to bumper stickers. Even though there is big money to be made in Elvis souvenirs, a spokesperson says, "We are protective here of the peace and quiet. Our objective is to keep the tremendous appeal, the charisma of the place where it started."

Busloads of Japanese and English fans come all summer. Some English fan clubs charter planes to make annual pilgrimages to Memphis, Nashville and Tupelo. English punk rockers, grandmothers from Georgia, middle-aged women from New Jersey, truck drivers from California, and the curious from everywhere come and go without disturbing the peace and quiet. They usually leave in a reflective mood. They may drive down the main street, see the hardware store where Elvis' family bought him his first guitar, and try to imagine what the little boy from the wrong side of town would say when he walked the same street.

Did he ever dream thousands of people would come to Tupelo each year, just because it was the city of his birth? Or that the same people would line up and pay money to walk through the house where he had spent the first three years of his life?

Was there any clue that the scruffy, towheaded youngster was bound for fame and fortune? No. Elvis was just one of hundreds of poor white youngsters with no discernible future in his hometown, that's why truck drivers stand in the front room of the house where he was born and cry. For one poor southern boy, the American dream came true.

Tupelo is located at the junction of US 45 and US 78 about 170 miles northeast of Jackson. Accommodations, fast food establishments and restaurants are plentiful in town.

Elvis Presley's birthplace is located at 306 Elvis Presley Drive just off US 78 East. The visitor's center and chapel are opened from 10 a.m. to 5 p.m. Monday through Saturday and from 1 p.m. to 5 p.m. on Sundays from October through June 1. Summer hours are 9 a.m. to 5:30 p.m. Monday through Saturday and 1 p.m. to 5 p.m. on Sundays. Admission fee charged.

For more information about Tupelo and Elvis' birthplace, contact the Tupelo Convention and Visitors Bureau, P.O. Box 1485, Tupelo, MS 38802. Telephone 601-841-6521.

21
Columbus

Heros come in a variety of styles. There are swashbuckling military men, soft-spoken kind-hearted women, and people who in the course of ordinary events are never even noticed. Sometimes the heroic have curious backgrounds. Their pasts don't necessarily foretell their futures. Columbus, Mississippi, nurtures the memories of all types of heros. Number one on the list is Stephen D. Lee.

A native of Charleston, South Carolina, Lee did not move to Columbus until after the Civil War. Legends claim that Lee was one of the Confederate officers sent to demand the surrender of Fort Sumter in Charleston harbor back in April 1861. When the Union commander refused, the legend goes, Lee and his cohorts went back to the mainland and ordered the Confederate artillery on the shore battery to open fire.

He rose through the officer ranks of the Confederate army to lieutenant general before he reached his 30th birthday, living a simple life during military campaigns, never carrying more baggage than would fit behind his saddle, eating and sharing shelter with the common soldier. Jefferson Davis said he was, "one of the best all-round soldiers which the war has produced."

His mastery of logistics and organizational abilities were put to use in his new life in Mississippi when he became the first president of A&M College of Mississippi (Mississippi State University). The only surprise in the general's scenario is that he is remembered as a champion of women's rights.

His home, the Blewett-Lee House, circa 1847, built by Mrs. Lee's grandfather at 316 Seventh Street, was a legacy to the town and used for many years as part of a high school complex.

Now the old home shelters a museum on the second floor which displays General Lee's personal effects, family photographs, costumes and antebellum toys. Community meeting rooms are downstairs. The Italianate-styled mansion with its ancient brick exterior and lacy white wrought-iron porch trim sits on spacious grounds populated with antique ornamental animals made of steel.

Just as Columbus' heros come in wide varieties, so does the architecture. The red brick St. Paul's Episcopal Church, Second Avenue South, hints of an English design heritage. Completed in 1858, the quiet church boasts a Tiffany stained glass window. Next door, on the church grounds, the simple lines of a Victorian cottage embellished with lacy Gothic trim, refurbished in the yellow, grey and white colors of its period (circa 1876), overpowers the church with its aura of importance. This rectory was the birthplace of Pulitzer Prize-winning playwright Tennessee Williams in 1911. His grandfather was pastor at St. Paul's. Though the family moved away when Williams was just a toddler, many literary experts say Columbus is fictionalized as

Tennessee Williams' birthplace, Columbus.

"Blue Mountain," the hometown of Tom Wingfield's mother, Amanda, in *The Glass Menagerie*. The play recalls Amanda entertained "gentlemen callers" on the front porch of the rectory and Tom's father is "a telephone man who fell in love with long distances. . . ." Williams father, C. C., was a telephone company manager in Columbus before taking a position as a traveling salesman.

The rectory is now used for church offices. If the offices are open, the staff is usually happy to let visitors wander through the old house. A historic marker outfront notes the birth of Columbus' literary hero.

You can hardly go a block in the downtown area without seeing one or two antebellum or Victorian architectural beauties. The streets are numbered, not named, which can cause endless confusion, because the same numbers are used for streets and avenues. But bold adventurers who don't fear disorientation will be rewarded with glimpses of an original antebellum tin-roof painted red (Camellia Place, one block north of Blewett-Lee Home), a pioneer log cabin built in the early 1800s which later had a Greek Revival home built around it (Hickory Sticks, Lee Park), and eclectic combinations of such architectural styles as Greek Revival, Gothic, and Victorian (White Arches, 122 7th Avenue South and Shadowlawn, 1024 2nd Avenue South). Many of the homes are as elegant inside as out. Federal-styled Riverview, 514 2nd Street South, boasts a spiral stairway which curves, unsupported from the first floor main hall to the fourth floor observatory. Certain touches and flourishes on the antebellum mansions appear more reminiscent of Mobile than of other Mississippi cities. Columbus' ties with the Alabama city downstream via the Tombigbee go back to early steamboat days, when cotton from the rich black belt went to market at Mobile.

De Soto is said to have crossed the Tombigbee near Columbus in 1540. One early settler in the area, Gideon Lincecum, wrote of arriving in 1818 and discovering an old family friend (and distant relative) John Pitchlynn living nearby. Pitchlynn came to inspect Lincecum's homesite to see if it was out of the flood zone and would drain sufficiently. Pitchlynn lived among the Choctaw Indians, served as an interpreter for that nation in dealings with the U.S. government, and was the father of the Choctaw chief Peter Pitchlynn. A true frontier hero John Pitchlynn is said to have died at Waverly Plantation about 15 miles from the present-day city limits.

Columbus was first called Possum Town for the distinctive physical characteristics of one of the founding fathers, Spirus Roach, who arrived sometime between 1817–1819. But by 1821 new settlers had arrived from Virginia and North Carolina and they opted for the more dignified designation of Columbus. These more serious-minded citizens opened what may have been the first "free" school in the state, Franklin Academy, in 1821, on the corner of 3rd Avenue North and 5th Street—now the site of a modern elementary school. Even though it was free and public does not mean it was open to all. But it was a beginning that eventually did lead the town's citizens to bring educational opportunities to youngsters of all economic circumstances, sexes and races. Columbus Female Institute, 1848, was a forerunner of Mississippi University for Women which was founded as a state college for women in 1884.

Though the townspeople moved boldly forward on the educational front, they frowned on certain aspects of "progress." They refused to let the railroads come through town until 1861. They reasoned it would be a bad influence, bring undesirable people to town and "mar the landscape."

The Civil War's horrendous battle at Shiloh (April 1862) over 120 miles away produced so many wounded that thousands of casualties were sent to Columbus for care. Many public and private buildings became hospitals including Callaway Hall on the MUW campus. After the fall of Jackson to Union forces in 1863, the state government was moved here. The Christian Church next door to the courthouse became the senate chamber while the house of representatives met in the courthouse.

Jefferson Davis visited at that time. A guest at Snowdoun, 906 3rd Avenue North, he was roused from his sleep by cheering admirers one night, stepped out on the front balcony in his nightshirt and dressing gown and addressed the crowd.

Confederate graves and memorial, Friendship Cemetery, Columbus.

The Odd Fellows Cemetery, at the end of 4th Street South, became the burial ground of several thousand Confederate soldiers and about 40 Union soldiers. In 1866 local women visiting the graves of relatives lost in the war noticed how neglected and forgotten the graves of the Union soldiers were. In perhaps the most heroic move ever made in Columbus, the women rallied their female friends, neighbors and relatives. The group descended on the cemetery grooming and decorating the graves of all the Civil War dead—both Union and Confederate. Their compassionate deed touched the heart of the nation and their Decoration Day evolved into our national Memorial Day. In the process Odd Fellows Cemetery became Friendship Cemetery. The Union soldiers are gone now, removed to Arlington by the government they served. Most of the Southern dead are united with the earth they loved under markers bearing the inscription, "Unknown Confederate Soldier."

Columbus is located at the junction of US 82 and US 45 North in northeast Mississippi near the Alabama border. Accommodations, fast food establishments and restaurants are plentiful in town.

A "narrative map" in brochure form that outlines a 30-minute driving tour past many historic homes and points of interest is offered free of charge by the Chamber of Commerce, 318 7th Street North, Columbus, MS 39701. Some historic homes may be open throughout the year by appointments made through the Chamber of Commerce; write or telephone 601-328-4491.

Blewett-Lee Home, next door to the Chamber of Commerce at 316 7th Street, is open on Tuesday and Thursday afternoons, or at other times by appointment. Admission free.

22
Nanih Waiya, Cave Mound, Dancing Rabbit Creek

Nanih Waiya appears suddenly, rising out of the flat field like an apparition. You must ply a deliberate course, over twisting, narrow country roads to reach the great mound, and still when you see it for the first time, part of your mind says it's not real, it's a myth.

And it is. This is not just another trip, but a pilgrimage to the place where time began. This mythical mound of earth anchored so securely in the north central Mississippi farmland is the birthplace of "the people," the name by which American Indians almost always refer to themselves.

Long ago, in a shadowy memory world that no longer exists, Uncle John first told us the story of Nanih Waiya. After dinner on lazy, south Mississippi summer afternoons when we managed to escape the nap enforcers, we children would collect on the front porch, cluster around Uncle John's rocker and beg for a story. Through the thin gray smoke of his burning cigarettes, he could conjure up visions of far, distant and even mythical places that would hover in the thick, humid air until they vaporized and sunk so deep into our consciences that they became interwoven with our reality. Uncle John told us all about Nanih Waiya.

This is his version of the myth, acculturated, worn down by time and mingling cultures: Chickasaw and Choctaw, the twins, were the last born of mother earth's children. The firstborn twin Chickasaw struggled to his feet as soon as he was dry and walked away to seek a homeland. While Choctaw was still wet from the journey deep within the earth, while he was lying in the grass, drying in the sun, he heard Nanih Waiya crying. Through her tears mother earth called to her last born child.

"Don't leave me," she pleaded. All of her other children had left, now she was afraid, afraid of growing old alone. Choctaw promised his mother that he would never leave, that he would always stay nearby. And he did.

Uncle John's raspy, tobacco strained voice, summoned by the sight of Nanih Waiya, tells the story to my heart, again and again, each time I come here. This is where we commune across the mystic frontiers.

The wind's song is a private concert of gently moving leaves, as the breeze dances through the stands of hardwoods and pines guarding the nearby stream. The steep slopes of the mound will steal your breath, but you are guaranteed a fairly safe footing on the wooden scaffolding stairs the state park service has built up one side of the mound. No matter the time of year, whether the fields are freshly plowed in spring, or bursting with the rank growth of summer, or mellowed for the autumn harvest, or barren and fallow for the duration of the winter, the view from atop Nanih Waiya is special. Though it is no great mountain, you feel elevated, removed from the real world of towns and farm fields, transported into the world of myths and legends. All you need is your imagination to conjure up visions of long forgotten ceremonies moving through their own shadowy ritualistic detail. You can almost smell the smoke of the ancient Choctaw fires.

The state park service maintains a roadside park on MS 393 directly across the road from the mound. There is a picnic area, a park office and fishing area. Legend marks the Cave Mound as the very spot the Choctaw first emerged into this world. It's reached by a detour of several miles. Take 393 to Coy Methodist Church; signs from that point mark the way. The last portion of the road is unpaved. Cave Mound hides in the deep woods, surely still a temple, a place of worship for those who love nature. The mound's dimensions are gently worn by age. Hickory trees, oaks and a few pines cover the hill. Wildflowers carpet the earth. An observation deck has been built over the entrance to the actual cave on the far side of the mound, by the creek. A suspended footbridge across the creek leads to short woodland trails. Tables and cooking grills nestled under the

Nanih Waiya, the mythical birthplace of the Choctaw people.

trees make this a perfect secluded spot for a picnic.

Nanih Waiya is about 20 miles from Philadelphia's main Choctaw reservation. Out of Philadelphia take MS 21 northeast, then MS 393. Or from Macon take MS 14 west to MS 490 to 393. Nanih Waiya is about 25 miles southwest of Macon.

Macon's post office mural freezes forever the point in time the Indians, government officials and militia gathered at Dancing Rabbit Creek in 1830 to sign a treaty that would attempt to expel the Choctaw from their homeland and remove them from the comfort and nourishing arms of their mother. The mural portrays dark masses of Indians in the woods—as much a part of the wilderness as the trees. The signers are clustered in the center, dominated by sinister, specter-like white men; an expressionless Indian face frames the right, a surveyor holding his tripod frames the left. Empty whiskey jugs, broken pottery and gnawed bones are strewn about the ground.

The road to Dancing Rabbit Creek, MS 14 out of Macon, passes through Mushulaville (also spelled Mashulaville) about eight miles to the west, twisting and turning and looping back over nearly forgotten byways. The route is intricate. Settlers' log cabins, long since abandoned, with trees growing out of their interiors, add to the poignancy of the trip into the peaceful, quiet countryside. Deep within the deserted country the modern road crosses the ancient Six Towns Trail, an Indian route from the Chickasaw nation to Mobile that linked Native American communities before the white man came.

Dancing Rabbit Creek's treaty is commemorated with a tombstone styled monument in the middle of a Choctaw graveyard. The slight knoll, down a dusty, red clay road, is encircled with common wire fencing. The gate is made of unfinished saplings. The markers on many of the Choctaw graves are simple hunks of red stone. The tall pines offer shelter to the memory of departed spirits as well as the wounded souls who linger here.

Delicate and tenacious wildflowers break through the thick, jungle-like tangle of undergrowth surrounding the graveyard fence.

The silence of elapsed time has erased the traces of the noisy encampment, where about 6000 Choctaw and what historians call a "numerous amount" of unsavory white people (gamblers, saloon keepers and speculators of all kinds) as well as government officials gathered for what turned into a carnival for most of the assembled. But the laughter, partying, fiddles and jigs have long been forgotten. If anyone thinks the Indians got a fair deal, their voices are seldom audible.

A cardinal darts through the pines, a red flag to warn those who linger too long in these deep woods. This place belongs to the past. We are spiritual trespassers.

The Mississippi Band of Choctaw Indians operate a museum at their reservation headquarters near Philadelphia, Mississippi. Artifacts and films tell the story of the modern Choctaw and their ancestors. Visitors are welcome.

Nanih Waiya is located about 20 miles from the Mississippi Band of Choctaw Indians Reservation at Philadelphia. From Philadelphia take MS 21 northeast, then MS 393. The highway literally runs through the park. To reach Cave Mound take MS 393 from Nanih Waiya to Coy Methodist Church; signs from that point mark the way. The last portion of the road is unpaved. The gates to the unpaved road open at 9 a.m. and close at 5 p.m.

Macon is located just off US 45 on MS 14. The post office is on Jefferson Street.

The route to Dancing Rabbit Creek: from Macon take MS 14 West, at Mushulaville take MS 490, about three miles turn left, follow signs to treaty ground. About three more miles, still following the signs (which are sometimes difficult to see), turn left on dirt road. Follow this road for about one mile. You'll cross what appears to be a logging trail (once the trail to Six Towns); pass a few houses and then on a slight rise, a cemetery, deep in the pines, will be on your right.

The Choctaw Museum of the Southern Indian is located within the Mississippi Band of Choctaw Indians' reservation compound near the tribal offices just off MS 16 west of Philadelphia. Telephone 601-656-5251. Open year round, but hours vary. Call first.

Admission free at all sites.

Accommodations are available at Philadelphia. Restaurants are scarce in the area. Restrooms and picnic facilities are at Nanih Waiya and Cave Mound.

23
Meridian

Painted ponies, goats, deer, lions and tigers run in an endless circle of joy for the children of Meridian. Since 1909 the city's youngsters have found happiness on the Highland Park Carousel. Circus music drifts out from the carousel house mingling with the aroma of popcorn, cotton candy and the laughter of children. This is where visitors can catch a glimpse of Meridian's soul.

A gung-ho modern city, continually pushing and stretching its boundaries physically, spiritually and economically, Meridian is doing what many cities are afraid can't be done—moving into a sleek, upbeat, high tech future while fully embracing the past. In this New South town, history is not a dirty word. The Highland Park Carousel and the generations of children who have ridden its circle continuously since 1909 are symbolic of how townspeople have had an ongoing relationship with the town's heritage.

Government, administrative and business offices as well as retail establishments are at home and thriving in the downtown area of post-Civil War Victorian and turn-of-the-century buildings. The Meridian Main Street Program and the Meridian Historical Preservation Commission have published a Historical Walking Tour of the downtown area that is easy to follow and offers a close-up inspection of period architecture. Street vendors in colorful festooned carts hawk hot dogs, soft drinks and other munchables along the route on weekdays.

Prior to the Civil War, Meridian was a small community at a railroad crossing. The war brought a Confederate arsenal, military hospital, prisoner-of-war stockade and headquarters for some state officials. Union Major Eli Lilly, a prisoner of war

taken by CSA General Nathan Bedford Forrest's troops, described Meridian at that time as "A forsaken hole of sand and
cabins." Perhaps a prejudiced view, but most of whatever was
Meridian was swallowed up by the fires Union General William
Tecumseh Sherman's troops set on one of their famous destructive marches. After Sherman's 10,000-man army had finished
ripping up the railroads for miles around, the general proclaimed, "Meridian . . . no longer exists." But as soon as he
marched on, repairs started and in about a month the tracks
were reopened.

The railroad assured the rebirth of Meridian. Reconstruction
era riots, epidemics, tornadoes and fires only caused momentary
lapses in the city's growth. The present passenger depot was
built in 1906 and is now an Amtrak station. How deep does the
love of railroading run here? This is the town that spawned the
singing brakeman, the father of country music, the blue-
yodeller—Jimmie Rodgers.

The Jimmie Rodgers Museum, housed in a building resembling an early railroad depot, displays his personal effects,
guitars, and music as well as a video-documentary of his life. In
the six years before his death in 1933, Rodgers recorded 110
songs.

The Jimmie Rodgers Museum is located in Highland Park
near the carousel. The park itself is historic. Called a "pleasure
park" it was of the type instituted by streetcar companies to
encourage extra traffic to travel to the end of the line. Highland
Park, circa 1903, has many of its original features and attractions which are now being restored and preserved. Just below a
ridge that played host to a Civil War skirmish, the 32-acre park
features on-going series of community concerts at the band-
stand, plus regular arts and crafts shows. The third weekend of
every month, antique dealers converge on the park for a show
and sale.

But nothing outshines the carousel, a true work of art built
by Gustav Dentzel of Philadelphia, Pennsylvania, between 1892
and 1899 for the St. Louis Exhibition. The city fathers bought
the carousel for $2000 in 1909 and built a carousel house to
shelter it. The carousel house is considered a rare architectural

Painted carousel pony, Highland Park, Meridian.

survivor, while no one doubts the carousel itself is a one-of-a-kind masterpiece. All the animals are hand-carved from poplar, apple and basswood. A menagerie carousel of this type pre-dates the all horse and pony styles. There are 21 Dentzel carousels left in the nation, but the Highland Park carousel is one of only three survivors of the earliest styles. It is considered the "purest" because it still has all its original animals. Sixty-four original oil paintings, all museum quality, by the Italian painter Salvatore Cernigiaro adorn the upper (outer and inner) circles of the carousel above the animals. The paintings on the outer circle are on wood, while on the inner circle, pictures are on canvas. A ticket to ride the carousel costs 25 cents. Orig-inally tickets cost a nickel. The original ticket booth with its circus coloring is in place as well as the concession stand with its popcorn and cotton candy. Local citizens never tire of visiting the carousel. Many stage special events here—every-thing from weddings to cocktail parties for visiting business people.

Meridian's most unexpected attractions are the burial sites of the "king and queen" of the gypsies. Shrouded in mystery the events that brought the queen here for burial in 1915 are not known. There is speculation that it was simply near the site where she died. The king later chose to be buried near his wife, as have several other members of the tribe. Jack Shank in his first volume of the history of Meridian, *The Queen with a Past,* writes that the queen (with the un-Romany name of Kelly Mitchell) "was laid out in her Romany finery, fine jewelled combs and a priceless gold coin necklace." He goes on to say since she was queen of all the gypsies in North America, she laid in state for 12 days while the tribe waited for members from all across the nation to assemble. And when the hearse headed out to Rose Hill Cemetery, it is estimated as many as 5,000 gypsies followed on foot. Now, the king, Emil Mitchell, rests beside his queen. All the gypsy graves are visited fre-quently by transient members of the tribe. Gifts of fresh fruits, fruit juices and flowers are left on the graves. The gypsies' plot is at the crest of Rose Hill. Rose Hill Cemetery is located at the western end of 7th Street.

Causeyville store, near Meridian.

Meridian serves a large trade area in Mississippi and Alabama. Causeyville is typical of rural communities serviced by the city. But the Causeyville General Store probably isn't at all typical of modern country stores. (To reach the store take MS 19 south, then follow the signs on the Meridian-Causeyville Road.) Stocked to the rafters with groceries and a microwave for warming ready-made commercial sandwiches, the store is also an unusual arena for a display of antique player pianos. Next door is an antique shop and a grist mill where local folks come on Saturday mornings to have their corn ground.

Going out of town on MS 39 to the north about 16 miles at Daleville is a monument to one of Mississippi's most famous pioneers, Sam Dale. Dale's homestead and grave were near the present-day Lizelia community. His remains were moved here in 1965. Also near Lizelia on Lizelia Road, in one of farmer Roy Frederickson's cow pastures, is what experts from the Smithsonian Institution say is the site of the Choctaw town Coosa. Pushmatha, the famous Choctaw chief, and his nephew Oklahoma once lived in Coosa. There is no marker at the site.

Merrihope, a Victorian era mansion, remodeled in the Colonial Revival style in 1904, furnished with Empire style antiques, and the Keys Aviation Museum which celebrates the world records set by the Key brothers here in the 1930s round out Meridian's current list of historic attractions. Meridian's Lauderdale County Department of Archives and History, located in the courthouse annex, is making giant strides in locating and marking "forgotten" sites as well as preserving documents and records. The area holds great promise for history lovers hungry for lost pages of the state's past.

Meridian is located in east central Mississippi near the Alabama border at the junction of I-20 and I-59. US 45 also passes through the town.

Highland Park, 19th Street and 41st Avenue. (Off I-20 and I-55, follow signs to Jimmie Rodgers' Museum.) Admission free. Telephone 601-485-1801.

Jimmie Rodgers Museum, Highland Park. Open year round. Telephone 601-485-1808. Addmission fee charged.

Carousel, Highland Park—25 cents per ride. Open daily May till September, then on weekends.

Meridian Main Street Program, P.O. Box 1986, Meridian, MS 39302. Telephone 601-485-1997. Offers walking tour map, free.

Rose Hill Cemetery is located on the western end of 7th Street. Admission free.

Causeyville General Store—take MS 19 south, follow the signs along the Meridian-Causeyville Road. About 12 miles from town. Admission free.

Sam Dale Monument is on MS 39 about 16 miles north of town. Admission free.

Merrihope, 905 Martin Luther King Avenue, Meridian, MS 39302. Telephone 601-483-8439. Admission fee charged.

Key Brothers Aviation Museum is located at the airport, Key Field. Open year round. Take airport exit from Interstates 59 and 20. Telephone 601-482-0364. Admission free.

For more information contact the Lauderdale County Tourism Commission, 2118 Front Street, P. O. Box 5866, Meridian, MS 39301. Telephone 601-483-0083.

24
Laurel—Lauren Rogers Museum of Art

Tucked away like a secret treasure hidden in the pine woods, the Lauren Rogers Museum of Art is symbolic of Laurel's second set of founding father's desire to create a cultivated society in their New South. Laurel began as a rough-hewn lumber camp in the early 1880s. An influx of tough dealing, would-be timber barons and lumberjacks gave the place a less than refined atmosphere. Then about 1890 a group of wealthy northern businessmen purchased the lumber camp and surrounding timberlands. Laurel became a company town. Lumberjacks and sawmill hands were encouraged to spruce up their cabins, go to church and send their children to such activities as piano lessons.

In the late 1920s and 1930s the small town had the only full-fledged art museum in Mississippi. Today housed in a neo-Georgian building on a posh and prosperous Victorian era street that has never needed restoring, the Lauren Rogers Museum of Art shelters works by Winslow Homer, George Inness, John Singer Sargent, Jean Francois Millet, John Sloan, Mary Cassat and Anna Mary Robertson "Grandma" Moses—just to name a few.

"Privately and generously endowed" according to a spokesman, the museum is not plagued with the financial worries that often can cripple such institutions. The museum began as a library which was erected as a memorial to Lauren Eastman Rogers, who died in 1922 following an appendectomy.

Rogers, 23, had just graduated from Princeton University, returned home, married and taken his place in the family lumber business. The young man's unfinished home site, on an oak-lined street that is more reminiscent of prosperous and prim New England than a small southern town, was the location chosen by his grandparents for a library to be built in his memory.

The library opened in 1923 and almost immediately the

Lauren Rogers Museum of Art, Laurel.

museum, containing seven exhibition rooms, was begun. In the early 1980s a new wing was added, and in 1983 the Lauren Rogers Library and Museum of Art became the Lauren Rogers Museum of Art. The library is still an important part of the museum. The fine arts book collection reflects the development of the museum collection, and special emphasis is placed on local history and genealogical materials.

In addition to American and European galleries with their collections of paintings, furniture and other pieces of decorative art, the English Gallery contains the Gibbons Georgian Silver Collection, and the Basket Rooms contain over 600 baskets from American Indian and other cultures collected and donated by Mrs. Catherine Marshall Gardiner of Laurel.

The Gardiner Basket Collection has been named "the best in a small museum east of the Mississippi" by Dr. Frederick Dockstader, former director of the Hay Foundation, Museum of the American Indian, New York City. The rarest and most valuable piece in the collection is a "jewel" basket made of woodpecker, meadowlark and quail feathers and used for ceremonial purposes by the Pomo, a southwestern tribe. The oldest examples of basketry in the collection are from the 18th dynasty of ancient Thebes. A bowl-shaped basket and sandal on display came from a mummy's tomb and are about 2000 years old. The oldest North American piece is an 800-year-old water jar from the southwestern U.S. Pueblo tribe. The tightly woven basket was coated with pitch to make it water tight. Apache granary baskets in the collection have been classified by Dr. Dockstader as the "finest anywhere."

The most romantic piece in the collection is a basket tray woven by the real-life Ramona who inspired Helen Hunt Jackson's novel of the same name. The star design on the tray is said to represent the soul of Ramona's departed husband.

The eclectic nature of the collections has embraced the interests of many patrons over the years. The nucleus of the museum's permanent collection was purchased by Lauren Eastman, Rogers' grandfather, for his home and reflects the personal tastes of the wealthy lumberman. Combined with other acquisitions made over the years, the collection has representative works from all the major movements and periods of American art as well as some European and Japanese pieces. The history of American art can be well illustrated with the museum's collections.

The warm ambience of the wood paneled library, the long booklined entrance to the galleries, the appointments and decorative touches from wrought-iron entrance gates, to a knight in armor, to a slick black marble staircase, give the visitor an illusion of not only viewing art, but moving inside an art piece as well.

The Lauren Rogers Museum of Art is located at the corner of Fifth Avenue and Seventh Street in downtown Laurel. The museum has its own exit signs off I-55. US 84 and MS 15 are also major routes through Laurel. The museum is closed on Mondays, Address: P.O. Box 1108, Laurel, MS 39440. Telephone 601-649-6374. Admission free.

Accommodations, restaurants and fast food establishments are plentiful in town.

25

Ellisville—The Free State of Jones

Stories of the Free State of Jones, the Mississippi county that supposedly seceded from the Confederacy during the Civil War, grow more illusive and fantasy-laden as time softens the jagged ridges of fact. Around the turn-of-the-century several noted southern historians declared that there had never been a Free State of Jones, a Jones Republic or any semblance of a government entity to fit the legends spun from a Confederate army deserter's antics during the Civil War. But despite the scholarly disclaimers, the stories endure. Could such stories exist without some fuel of truth?

If there had been a Free State of Jones, Ellisville would have been the capital. From here a group of yeoman farmers, scarcely a slave owner among the lot, sent a representative to the state assembly in 1861 with explicit orders to vote against secession. But once in Jackson the fellow succumbed to secession rhetoric and went against his instructions. Homefolks burned the representative in effigy. Many Jones County citizens rebelled against fighting a "planters' war." Others joined the Confederate forces. But many of those enlistees were quickly disillusioned when they learned if a man owned 20 or more slaves, he was excused from military service. So when a Jones County farmer named Newt Knight deserted the CSA, it could have been for philosophical reasons.

However, a kinswoman of the farmer/deserter, Ethel Knight wrote in her book, *The Echo of the Black Horn,* that Newt Knight deserted because he thought his wife was having an affair. For whatever reasons Newt Knight took to the tall pines and deep forest of Jones County and soon attracted a large band of fellow deserters who had returned to their homes from the "planters' war." The Confederate army made numerous attempts to capture the deserters but to no avail. Knight traveled to New Orleans, struck a deal with the Union forces there, became their agent/ally and returned to the Free State of Jones, not a Confederate deserter but an American patriot as far as Union forces were concerned. Legends persist that his stronghold, an island in the Leaf River, was a headquarters for a guerrilla army of 10,000 men. Magazine articles in the 1880s did much to enhance this tale.

Southern sympathizers remember Knight as an outlaw and renegade. Union Major Eli Lilly (who later founded the drug company) documented southern sentiment for Knight and his band during the war years. Taken prisoner by CSA General Nathan Bedford Forrest's forces, Lilly was sent to Meridian, then to Enterprise, Mississippi, where he said Union POWs were quartered in a warehouse and put on "parole of honor" not to leave the town limits. While the POWs were "relaxing in their quarters," Lilly related how a black boy raised the alarm, "The Republic of Jones is coming!"

Lilly, in his writings, described the Republic of Jones as having an independent government. The Union prisoners were led to believe that the Republic was a collection of outlaws and cut-throats who were coming to Enterprise for the expressed purpose of robbing the POWs—even though prisoners, the Union soldiers possessed money, watches and "good clothing." The local Confederate commander issued arms to the Union POWs until CSA troops could come up from Mobile to help defend the outpost. The POWs put pickets on the roads, loosened boards on the bridge leading to town so they could be taken up if it became necessary to pull back into town, set up defenses and waited. But though the Republic's forces came into full view, they didn't attack. Lilly believed the town to be full of the Republic's informants. The CSA troops arrived from Mobile, but they let the Union POWs continue on picket duty for several more days.

This unusual event can be interpreted several ways. Did the CSA commanders from Mobile leave the Union POWs in defense positions because they knew the strength of the Jones

A Confederate monument now sits on the courthouse square in Ellisville, Jones County. The county was known as the Free State of Jones and a hotbed of Union sympathizers during the Civil War.

Republic's Union alliance and believed they would not risk attacking the town if it meant harming or fighting Union soldiers? Some people chose to believe the incident points to the fact that the Republic practiced such atrocities that warring armies could temporarily unite against them.

Immediately after the war about 100 citizens of Ellisville and Jones County petitioned the state government to have the name of their county changed to Davis and their county seat to Leeville to help put the hateful memory of the Free State of Jones behind them. But according to local stories, Newt Knight and his followers controlled the government under federally imposed martial law and Reconstruction.

A trip to the Free State of Jones takes as many detours through musty records as it does down dusty country roads. The pine woods, the Leaf River and Tallahalla Creek swallow up man-made monuments and artifacts with awesome determination. These natural forces were the allies of Newt Knight. Now they are the allies of those who chose to forget. Knight spent his last days in the area around Soso, a town on MS 28 in northeast Jones County. People there still caution visitors not to ask "too many" questions.

In Ellisville a ghostly reminder of Newt Knight appears occasionally on the dining room floor of the Isacc Anderson house at the corner of Anderson and Deason Streets, across the street from the local elementary school. A Confederate officer sent to capture Knight was a guest in the house when he was murdered. Supposedly on unpredictable occasions the blood stain reappears on the dining room floor where the mortally wounded rebel officer fell. The Anderson house, a private home, is sometimes open for tours during special local events.

The Anderson house as well as the older sections of the town give a romantic illusion of a lazy little village lost in a daydream, the newer section, especially between US 11 and I-59 jolts visitors back into the bustling traffic of modern enterprises. The old town near the courthouse square deserves a leisurely stroll. The rambling old houses, with the twists and turns of additions, the ambience of cozy bays and stained glass, the well-shaded yards, the white spire of a church, all frame a state of mind that makes the solitary monument to the Confederate dead on the courthouse lawn especially poignant.

Ellisville is located about 20 miles northeast of Hattiesburg and about seven miles southwest of Laurel on US 11 and I-59.

Some restaurants and fast food establishments are located in town. Accommodations are plentiful in both Laurel and Hattiesburg.

For information about the area and special local events, contact the Ellisville Chamber of Commerce, P.O. Box 280, Ellisville, MS 39437. Telephone 601-477-8617.

26
Jackson—The Capital City

Sunday afternoon is the best time for exploring Jackson. The quiet streets and uncrowded parking lots enhance the appreciation of the city's historical significance as well as invoke the image of less hurried times.

The city gained the position of repository for state history when it became the capital of Mississippi in the 1820s. Before then the town site was known as LeFleur's Bluff in honor of the adventurous French-Canadian Louis LeFleur who operated a trading post here. He is remembered best as the father of Greenwood Leflore, the legendary Choctaw chieftain.

In territorial days Natchez and its neighboring town Washington had served as seats of government, and Columbia, Marion County, was temporarily capital before the move to this more central location on the Pearl River. A statue of Andrew Jackson, the American patriot for whom the city was named, graces the grounds of City Hall. A building of stark white southern elegance, City Hall is one of the few antebellum architectural survivors of the Civil War. During the tumult Union troops torched the city and reduced the proud community with its checkboard ratio of parks, greens and buildings to a series of ruins nicknamed "Chimneyville."

Though many records and documents of the state's early days were destroyed or lost during the war, the State House, or Old Capitol, as it is known today, survived. Officially the State Historical Museum, the proud old building at the foot of East Capitol Street opens doors to the corridors of the past. The Greek Revival styled capitol was architecturally and spiritually a temple of government. The legislative chambers, the rotunda, the galleries and even the stairwells have heard the political secrets, scandals and deals that shaped the state's destiny from 1839 until 1903. In these halls the first law in the US to recognize the property rights of married women passed in 1839. A remarkable piece of legislation, probably the most significant ever enacted here, the law drew on the customs and traditions of Native Americans as opposed to prevailing English Common Law.

Andrew Jackson addressed the legislature here in 1840, the year the building was pronounced "finished." The legislature had started meeting in the building a year earlier. Henry Clay addressed Mississippians and was treated to a reception here in 1843. And at the close of the Mexican War, Jefferson Davis brought his band of Mississippi volunteers to the capitol and addressed crowds of Jacksonians from the second story balcony. The Ordinance of Secession was passed here in 1861. At the end of the war, Federal troops arrested the governor in these same halls. A conspiracy to forget surrounds most of the Reconstruction governors and legislatures. The last of the Reconstruction governors left office under threat of impeachment in 1876. Jefferson Davis returned to address the legislature in 1884.

Now, museum exhibits grapple with the chronology and scope of the state's history in the Old Capitol. Sharing the same block, Capitol Green, is the Mississippi War Memorial Building and the Charlotte Capers Building (State Department of Archives and History). The War Memorial, built in 1940, around an open courtyard, houses the Mississippi Military Museum, a three-dimensional presentation of US military history from the Spanish-American War to the Vietnam Conflict. Featured are a 13 foot scale model of the World War II battleship, the USS Mississippi, a weapons collection, uniforms and a shrine to Mississippians who have earned the Congressional Medal of Honor.

At the opposite end of Capitol Green the State Archives house surviving and salvaged bits of the state's history—from official government documents to personal letters to photographs and various other types of records made over the years.

"Old" Capitol in Jackson is also known as the State Historical Museum.

The monument directly in front of the Archives honors Confederate soldiers of Mississippi and was dedicated June 3, 1891, the anniversary of Jefferson Davis' birth. A statue of Davis was originally located within the monument.

In 1903 the New Capitol Building, built to resemble the National Capitol, was completed on the site where the state penitentiary had stood. Legends claim that the old prison walls were so stout that they could not be torn down in spots, and portions are still standing within the mound-like rise on the grounds of the opulent New Capitol. More than 15 types of marble plus the luster of generous amounts of gold leaf and the sheen of well polished oak, maple, walnut and mahogany decorate the corridors and chambers where Mississippi's law-makers gather annually. Outside, a dome 180 feet from ground level is crowned with an eight-foot eagle with a wing spread of 15 feet. Made of copper coated with gold-leaf, the great bird faces south. For many years the golden eagle dominated the Jackson skyline.

The Governor's Mansion, built in 1842, is just up the street a few blocks from the Old Capitol and was designed by that building's architect, William Nichols. Surrounded by modern buildings and hectic business enterprises, the mansion and grounds are an antebellum island of trees, flowers and disarming quiet in downtown Jackson. The governor's official residence is one of the oldest executive mansions in the U.S. to be continually occupied. The mansion did hospital duty during the Civil War and was the scene of a victory dinner hosted by Union General W. T. Sherman after the fall of Vicksburg in 1863.

Reflecting a totally different architecture and lifestyle, the Manship House, circa 1857, was the home of the Civil War mayor of the city. Charles Henry Manship, an ornamental painter by trade, brought his artistic expertise and craft into full play in the decorations he devised for his Gothic Revival cottage. Manship is remembered more for his house than for the fact that he surrendered the city to General Sherman. Examples of Manship's ornamental painting survive in the house, and have been restored. Some of the original wallpaper, which may have come from Manship's shop, has been uncovered and reproduced. The cottage, containing three bedrooms, parlor, sitting room, dining room and bathing room, is furnished as a southern home of its type would have been in 1888.

The Civil War often seems to overshadow Jackson's past. There is a pragmatic legacy behind the names Fortification Street and Battlefield Park. But there is more depth and breadth to Jackson's past than a glimpse from a single event or perspective will allow.

Jackson and Mississippi's heritage from another point of view can be explored at the Smith Robertson Museum and Cultural Center. The experience of black Mississippians as well as their heritage and roots are explored through exhibits and displays at the museum. The first public school for blacks in Jackson, the school had its beginnings in 1894. The Art Deco building where the museum is housed was constructed in 1929. The museum offers an opportunity to venture into a world of culture and traditions seldom available.

Jackson at the junction of I-55 and I-20 and highways US 49 and US 80 is in the west central portion of the state. Accommodations, restaurants and fast food establishments are plentiful.

City Hall, President Street at Pearl Street. Telephone 601-960-1530. Open daily. Admission free.

Old Capitol Museum, 100 South State Street at the foot of East Capitol. Telephone 601-354-6222. Open Monday through Friday 8 a.m. to 5 p.m. Saturday from 9:30 a.m. to 4:30 p.m. Sunday 12:30 p.m. to 4:30 p.m. Admission free.

War Memorial Building, 120 North State Street. Telephone 601-354-7207. Open Monday through Friday 8:30 a.m. to 4:30 p.m. Admission free.

Governor's Mansion, 300 E. Capitol Street, Telephone 601-354-7650. Free tours by appointment Tuesday through Friday.

State Capitol (New Capitol), High Street. Telephone 601-354-7294. Open for tour by appointment daily. Admission free.

Manship House, 420 East Fortification Street, Telephone 601-961-4724. Monday through Friday 8 a.m. to 5 p.m. Saturday 9:30 a.m. to 4:30 p.m. Sunday 12:30 p.m. to 4:30 p.m. Admission free.

Smith-Robertson Museum and Cultural Center, 528 Bloom Street (near New Capitol). Telephone 601-960-1457. Hours 9 a.m. to 5 p.m. Monday through Friday, Saturday and Sunday by appointment. Admission free.

27
Jackson—Mississippi's Agriculture and Forestry Museum

The farmer's wife sweeps her yard clean with a homemade broom, plucking up every blade of grass before it scarcely pokes its way through the hard dirt outside her front door. Often as not in the summertime, she's barefoot and amuses herself by singing a hymn while she works.

Stop at the end of the lane and say hello. When she looks up from her chore, smiles and says, "Oh, hi, come on in," and opens the gate, you cross over the edge of reality into her world.

Her world of transposed time and place somewhere shortly after the First World War in rural Mississippi now exists only in the confines of the Mississippi Agriculture and Forestry Museum.

The museum staff has re-created and preserved a piece of this distant world by moving the Fortenberry-Parkman Farm (1860–1960) from Pearl River County to urban Jackson. The farm has been restored to its 1920 appearance and all log structures (besides the cabin and barn, there are sheds, smokehouses and corncribs) are preserved and restored to the manner in which they were constructed in 1860. The kitchen and several out buildings were constructed with lumber about 1880.

The cabin's main room is a living room-bedroom. An open walkway connects the cabin with the kitchen and dining room. Costumed interpreters portray the farmer and his wife. They talk to visitors while continuing with their chores on the farm. In the morning visitors are asked to sit a spell at the dining table and enjoy a biscuit fresh from the wood cookstove's oven. There's real butter for the biscuits on the table under a piece of cheese cloth and there's blue ribbon cane syrup in the can if you feel like dribbling a sticky trickle across your butter-smeared bread. In the afternoons visitors are offered teacakes, also fresh from the oven.

A flock of chickens cluck around the kitchen steps and the farmer's wife tosses them any crumbs she might wipe from the table. She washes dishes in an enamel basin and when she is done, throws the dirty water out the back door in a grand splash the chickens scurry to flee. It can't get more authentic than this.

In the proper seasons there are crops in the fields and there is always a bevy of farm animals for the farmer to tend and the visitors to see up-close.

A small crossroads town, circa 1920, is near the farm. Some buildings were constructed on site, but most are "real" buildings moved onto the museum grounds from their original locations throughout the state. A church, schoolhouse, doctor's office, general store, gas station, sawmill, cotton gin, cane mill for syrup making, blacksmith shop and gristmill manned by costumed interpreters and craftsmen give visitors a clear picture of the lifestyles enjoyed in small Mississippi villages in earlier times. There are also the more typical museum displays and exhibits, inside a massive building on the grounds.

A division of the Mississippi Department of Agriculture and Commerce, the museum was conceived as a place where visitors could get a look at the economic history of the state and its impact on culture and lifestyle. The exhibits tell the story of Mississippi from the native forest dependency of Indians in pre-Columbian times to modern farmers with crop-dusting airplanes.

Indians, Spanish and French explorers, lumbermen, share-croppers and truck farmers are all chronicled along with the tools of their various trades. But the real hero of the museum is the yeoman farmer and it is his story the exhibits tell best. Usually unsung heros, the yeoman farmers moved onto the Mississippi frontier in search of self-sufficiency and independence. They were the men whose legacy cuts across all racial and ethnic lines to give many modern day Mississippians souls

In living history demonstrations at the Agriculture and Forestry Museum (Jackson), an actress portraying a farmer's wife feeds a flock of chickens at the kitchen door of the farmhouse.

and spirits that still yearn for independence. Unfortunately, the yeoman farmers are the men whose stories usually get lost in the shuffle of Mississippi history.

The glamourous pre-Civil War plantation lifestyles romanticized in fiction and film, the opulent era of great houses and staggering wealth enjoyed by a scant handful of Mississippians, lasted for just a short time. The history of the people is the history of the yeoman farmer. The heart of the museum's 39-acre site is the Fortenberry-Parkman Farm, a real working yeoman farm for a solid 100 years.

The Mississippi Agriculture and Forestry Museum is located in Jackson at 1150 Lakeland Drive. Telephone 601-354-6113. Open year round. Hours 9 a.m. to 5 p.m. Monday through Saturday and 1 p.m. to 5 p.m. Sundays. Closed major holidays. Admission fee charged.

Accommodations, restaurants and fast food establishments are plentiful in Jackson.

28
Vaughan—Casey Jones Museum

Casey Jones was a traveling man. He had logged so many thousands of miles by April 29, 1900, at the throttles of the fast moving steam trains of the Illinois Central Railroad that he had become a legend.

Casey cut through the distances, rolling across the south, playing his steam whistle (The Whippoorwill) with such style that even people in the smallest and most remote southern towns knew when he was passing through.

On April 29, 1900, Casey chugged into Memphis aboard his new locomotive, No. 382, at 8:20 p.m.—right on time. When he checked-in he learned the engineer scheduled to take the "Cannonball" south to Canton, Mississippi, was ill and unable to make the run. Casey said, "No problem" and agreed to substitute as long as his fireman Sim Webb would come along also.

The two men hooked up No. 382 to six cars of the New Orleans Special, the Cannonball, and at 12:50 a.m. started south. The Cannonball was 95 minutes behind schedule. Casey said that was no problem either. He'd make up the lost time and arrive at Canton, 190 miles away, on time.

At Grenada, Mississippi, Casey got the word that six trains operating south of Memphis would soon be converging at Vaughan to be sorted and rerouted. But by the time he arrived the track should be clear.

It was going to take some doing. There would still be two long trains at Vaughan. There was a passing track and a house track at the Vaughan depot and with some careful calculating and some "sawing," an intricate maneuver which called for a train to move up the side track and be partially on the main

141

track to the south while Casey and the Cannonball cleared the northern end—then immediately back up and be off the southern end of the main track by the time No. 382 would reach it—everything would be fine.

There wasn't a lot of maneuvering room either on the track or the clock. As the longest train started down the passing track to begin the "sawing," an air hose ruptured and the loss of pressure automatically locked the brakes on the freight train leaving three cars and a caboose out on the main track.

A flagman was dispatched up the track to warn oncoming trains and Casey of the situation. But the Cannonball thundered by the flagman at more than 75 mph. By the time Casey heard the sharp crack of the warning torpedoes, the flagman had placed on the tracks just north of Vaughan, time had run out.

Casey hit the brake and ordered the fireman to jump. He was able to slow the Cannonball down to 40 mph before it crashed into the freight train's caboose and three cars loaded with hay and corn and overturned.

None of the people in the four passenger cars were hurt. Fireman Webb's injuries netted him $5 compensation from the

Casey Jones Museum, Vaughan.

ICRR. Casey died. His death is considered such a heroic act, it is still remembered today as a noble sacrifice.

The song "Casey Jones" has probably done more to spread Casey's fame than the act that inspired the lyrics. The song was written by Wallace Saunders, a black man from Canton. He received scant recognition and no money for his effort.

Here in the Casey Jones Museum the song plays almost continuously. Models of railroads, trains and assorted memorabilia line the walls and fill display cases in the Vaughan Museum Depot.

The old Vaughan depot, the one Casey never reached, rotted and was torn down. But according to a spokesman for the Mississippi Department of Natural Resources, the museum is actually the last depot Casey passed back on April 30, 1900. It was moved here from Pickens.

A national historic site marker has been placed between the highway and the railroad track. Mrs. Casey Jones and Sim Webb came down to the dedication in 1953.

Most of the town of Vaughan is state park property. There is an old drug store, post office and movie house that may eventually be restored.

Rose Rest, a boarding house where railroad employees stayed and/or ate, is slowly being engulfed by time. There is hope someone will see the potential of a restored "bed and breakfast" establishment in the rambling old house.

Once a bustling small town where cotton buyers converged and the Saturday night dance was always "the" social event, Vaughan has dwindled to the park buildings, Rose Rest, a viable, privately owned general store and several homes.

The big event on Vaughan's social calendar now is the annual Hobo Day, the last Thursday of every September. All the self-confessed hoboes appearing at this event rode the rails, without the formality of purchasing a ticket, during the depression. According to their stories they were seeking jobs, work, a better life and sometimes simple adventure.

Vaughan's passing track has been taken up. But the main track still carries Illinois Central Gulf traffic, and passengers still can catch a fleeting glimpse of the little town from the windows of the fast moving Amtrak. And who knows? Maybe deep into the dark of a Mississippi night, just north of Vaughan, some railroading men still hear the cry of The Whippoorwill.

Vaughan is located about 14 miles north of Canton. To reach the town/park take I-55 to exit 133 and follow the signs. Open year round, but hours and days vary. Telephone 601-673-9864. Admission fee charged.

Accommodations, restaurants etc. are plentiful in Jackson about 30 miles to the south.

29
Flora

Flora, a farming community of broad meadows bordered by white wooden fences, about 20 miles north of Jackson, measures its history in millions of years. The only petrified forest in the eastern United States is here. Geologists say the stone trees in the forest are from 36 to 38 million years old.

Since white settlers first became aware of the ancient trees embedded in the earth here, they have been visiting the site. One of the first written notices of the forest was made by Benjamin Wailes, Mississippi's pioneering naturalist, in the mid-1800s. Tunica and Marksville Indians lived in the area in the 16th century. It is not too farfetched to imagine that they too knew of the stone trees. Probably the biggest congregation of people ever to assemble in and around the forest came in relatively modern times. During the Civil War on May 17, 1863, General Joe Johnston camped here with a Confederate force of 18,000 men. The Confederates were making an attempt to out-maneuver a Union army under the command of General U.S. Grant.

A few weeks later, on July 1, 1863, another Confederate force, this time of 10,000 men under General William Walker on their way to Vicksburg to help raise the seige, bivouacked here. They were running late. Vicksburg fell to the Union July 4, 1863.

Union soldiers fought their way through here on October 17, 1863, when General J. B. McPherson accompanied by an expeditionary force of 8,000 soldiers met "vigorous" resistance from a force of some 2000 Confederates in his attempts to reach Canton. His march stalled. Local historians say he retreated to Vicksburg. Then on March 2, 1864, General W. T.

Sherman and 20,000 Union soldiers camped here while on their "Meridian Expedition"—to cut a swath of destruction across the state. The green living forest has erased or buried evidence of the hostilities and encampments.

As calmer times returned the petrified forest began to attract scholarly and scientific attention. By 1932 the National Encyclopedia listed the forest as one of the six notable examples of petrified forests in the world.

The scenario scientists have constructed of the prehistoric times that brought the forest into being go something this: A great flood swept through the area 36 to 38 million years ago. The raging waters became rivers of destruction swirling across the landscape, uprooting whole forests of exotic trees in far distant locales and depositing them here in a mammoth log-jam. This area was lowland in ancient times, a place where shifting rivers spread sand and silt over plains and shores. The trees were preserved from further decay by quick burial in the sands and silts carried by the muddy waters. Petrification, or

Visitors can be swallowed up in the deep shadows of the Petrified Forest, Flora.

turning to stone, took place in the thousands of years the logs lay buried by gradual infiltration of minerals such as silica. Other minerals such as iron gave the logs the red-rust color they have today.

Ice Age winds blew a fine powdery-soft, beige-colored sand into the region from the west. Gradually the forest was buried in the finely sifted soil called "loess" which sometimes, even now, runs hundreds of feet deep. When the loess soil's outer crust was disturbed, the rain would dissolve it like so much powdered-sugar. Stone trees would emerge in torrential rains, only to disappear as a later storm washed the soil in a different direction.

At first scientists believed that as living trees, these pieces of ancient driftwood grew in areas far to the north. But more recent studies have identified the trees as types grown in tropical environments. The ancient trees are a jigsaw piece of an unending natural history puzzle.

Tons of petrified logs were hauled out of the forest and many others damaged before the R. J. Schabilion family acquired the property and opened it to the public as a park in 1963. The Mississippi Petrified Forest was designated a registered National Natural Landmark in 1966 by the National Park Service and is one of the relatively few privately owned National Landmarks. The National Park Service says the forest "possesses exceptional value in illustrating the natural history of the United States."

A green living forest shelters the resting place of the ancient stone trees. Paths through the forest are bordered by rustic rail fences. A printed trail guide explains marked points. Nature has sculpted a "frog" and a "caveman's bench" from the stone logs still in the positions where they were first found. Another hollowed out petrified log forms a natural den for rabbits and maybe an occasional fox.

Fossil trees resembling sequoia, maple, fir, plus a cone-bearing tree whose nearest counterpart now grows in northwest Africa and a broadleaved tree that closely resembles trees now growing in the Amazon basin are strewn about in a rock garden of nature's own design. The high hills and gullies sheltering the forest were created by natural and man-made erosion. There are spots called "the badlands" where early white settlers' plow furrows can still be seen in the fragile earth's surface.

The trail is about five blocks long. Most people spend about 30 minutes meandering along the marked paths. A museum, located at the entrance to the forest, displays fossils from ancient camels to plant leaves to prehistoric turtles. Nature's works of art, the delicate outlines of an unknown fish etched into stone, the tracks of a dinosaur pressed into rock tantalize the imagination.

A high rolling meadow across from the entrance to the forest has been outfitted with picnic tables where visitors are invited to extend their stays.

The Petrified Forest at Flora is located off US 49 about 20 miles north of Jackson. Well placed signs mark the way. Open daily, year round. Restrooms and picnic facilities. Address: P. O. Box 98, Flora, MS 39071. Telephone 601-879-8189. Admission fee charged.

Accommodations, restaurants and fast food establishments available in Jackson.

30
Piney Woods Country Life School

Twenty miles south of Jackson, US 49 runs past a dream, a small realm of white board fences, stout barns, tall pines and lush fields where a miracle thrives. A prosperous-looking farm would be miracle enough here in a region of poor unfertile soil, but it is only a small part of the dream-come-true sheltered within the boundaries of the Piney Woods Country Life School campus.

Laurence Jones set out to build a school here, a pragmatic institution that would balance academic knowledge with vocational skills. He met with his first three students on a log under a cedar tree in 1909. Today in the area adjoining the spot, the campus of a viable modern school stands. Still dedicated to pragmatic principles, the school has about 360 students in grades 1 through 12. Largely built by students over the years, Piney Woods has a rustic charm that obscures the obstacles overcome in its creation.

Fresh out of college with a desire to share the knowledge he had gained, Dr. Jones, as he is remembered, accepted the position of teacher at a small black school, the Utica Institute, Hinds County. The son of a hotel porter and seamstress, Jones had grown up in St. Joseph, Missouri, in relatively prosperous circumstances compared to the poor people, both black and white, he met in Mississippi in 1907. His maternal grandfather had started a school in Addison, Michigan, in 1849, that had been open to all regardless of sex, race, religion or poverty—a school where books were studied to aid learning the skills

Entrance to Piney Woods Country Life School.

necessary to make a living. Jones wanted to start the same sort of school in Mississippi.

Overcoming the suspicions of the country people, both black and white, took some doing. The black people were convinced that Jones, a foreigner to them, would swindle them out of the hard-earned dimes and nickels that he asked they donate for a school and go back north and leave them with neither money or school. With the backing of a few community leaders, both black and white, Jones began his school mainly with hope. An affluent black farmer donated forty acres (where the first class met) and Jones began.

Students learned to read and write, bake bread, make syrup and bricks, do carpentry work and any other chores that were necessary to keep the boarding school going. Since 1909 no student who has asked for admittance to the school has ever been turned away. Graduates leave the school with a positive attitude that never fails to enhance their respective careers.

Optimism didn't always come easy. The stories of Dr. Jones' struggle could fill volumes. The following is one of the more often told of his adventures. In the early years the young teacher often spoke at country churches. One Sunday afternoon about the time of World War I, Jones was speaking to a black congregation when a group of white boys happened to be passing by and overheard part of the motivational talk. They interpreted it to mean he was encouraging a black uprising and immediately reported to their elders. Before the afternoon was out Jones was atop a pile of pine knots under an oak's stout limbs with a noose around his neck. According to the story, just as the noose was being tightened and the wood readied for lighting, someone in the crowd decided it would be amusing for Jones to give another speech. Supposedly, Jones said a prayer, then began to speak, to tell the lynch mob of his work. He kept talking, perhaps with more optimism than ever, giving the lynch mob the same fund-raising speech he had lately been perfecting. He convinced the white mob not only to remove the rope from around his neck, but to pass the hat among themselves. The would-be-murderers-turned-benefactors collected $50 for Dr. Jones' school. Many of Jones' miracles are documented.

A museum on the Piney Woods campus, in Dr. Jones former home, chronicles the school's growth and the adventures the founder and teachers have encountered over the years in their efforts to keep the school open. Overlooking one of the campus' five lakes, the Grace Jones Log Cabin was built as a memorial to Dr. Jones' wife and houses a photographic display of the school's history. The cabin has been designated a museum for the vocational skills taught at the school in the early years. Piney Woods gained national recognition and financial support from touring choirs made up of students for many years. But the school's biggest boost nationally came in the 1950s when Ralph Edwards featured Jones on the *This is Your Life* television program. The national television appearance made many new friends and supporters for the school.

Jones died at the age of 93 in 1975. His grave is near the spot of the cedar tree where he first held classes. The ancient log cabin, pre-dating the Civil War, that he and his first students rescued from the wilderness for their first school building has been encased in brick on the modern 2000-acre campus.

From the rock garden to the amphitheater nestling in the dips and rises on the landscape, to the distinctive sculptures and imaginative art works decorating the campus, visitors can follow a network of signs encouraging positive thinking. The little signs with their positive thoughts and quotes could serve as Dr. Jones' legacy to all Mississippians. Those who knew Jones say two of his favorite quotes are: Booker T. Washington's "I have learned that success is to be measured, not so much by the position one has reached in life, as by the obstacles which he has overcome while trying to succeed" and Henry Thoreau's "If one advances confidently in the direction of his dreams and endeavors to live the life that he has imagined, he will meet with success unexpected in common hours. . . ."

For many years a simple sign announced the Piney Woods Country Life School on US 49 and invited all travelers to stop for a cool drink of water. The sign is gone, but the invitation is still open.

Piney Woods Country Life School is located on US 49 about 20 miles south of Jackson in the Piney Woods community of Rankin County.

Telephone 601-845-2214.

The museum is open from 9 a.m. to 3 p.m. Monday through Friday during the school term. Admission free.

Accommodations, restaurants and fast food establishments available in Jackson.

31
Columbia and Sandy Hook

The rains come. The river rises. The town floods. The news media descend on the watery environs like a commando squad. By car, boat and helicopter they come. Daring to go where no sane native would willingly venture. The civil defense director issues regular bulletins. His face, his words become the most documented in town, just as the ravages of the nearly annual flood waters become the story the world knows best about this bit of real estate along the southern stretch of the temperamental Pearl River.

But Columbia, the self-proclaimed city of charm, hometown of the legendary football player Walter Payton, has a drier side. In the throes of an unrainy spring, gripped by stout wisteria vines flaunting their purple pennants in the gentle breezes as they perfume the air, mother nature pushes all her favorite flower children to be all they can be. Azaleas, dogwoods, daffodils, tulips and all their blooming cousins smudge the landscape with color. In the park beside the library it's a good time for lingering along tree canopied walkways and indulging in the age-old custom of promenading.

The good life of a small southern town peeks out from behind the hedges and fancy low fences. The Marion County Courthouse sits like a proud monarch at the head of the main business district streets where merchants cater to a clientele of farmers, oilmen, jobbers, independent manufacturers and bevies of southern belles.

Hugh White, a governor of Mississippi and a pioneering mayor here, is remembered for his efforts to "balance agri-

153

culture with industry." His home, on Broad Street, a Spanish-styled villa in a setting of pines and southern flowers, is about a mile from the courthouse on old Highway 98.

This is the town where state officials tried to hang Tom Purvis after convicting him of murder in a well-publicized trial in 1908. Old-timers still love to tell the story that they were told as youngsters of how people poured into Columbia for the spectacle. The noose was slipped around his neck, the trap sprung, but the rope slipped over Purvis' head. A voice in the crowd shouted that it was an act of God, Purvis was proven innocent by divine intervenion. But the state's judges weren't so sure. Purvis was sent to the state prison farm to serve a life sentence, but 15 years into the term, another man, dying from a snakebite (he had allowed the snake to bite him to prove his closeness to God and immunity from death) confessed to the murder of which Purvis had been convicted. Purvis was released from prison and paid $5000 for his troubles. The facts of the Purvis case long ago slipped into the realms of myth and now the legend comes in many shades of detail and nuances of color—all delightfully entertaining.

If your appetite for storytelling is aroused, you might try lunch or dinner at Aletha's, a unique folk-restaurant. Aletha, a soft-spoken black lady whose life is the stuff of epic sagas, always finds the universal truths in her own background to tie all our very human experiences together. Finding her restaurant is an adventure in itself. Take US 98 West through town across the bridge (the Pearl River), turn left at the state highway department building. Go back towards the river on the frontage road, take the first right, you'll see the railroad tracks to your left. Take the first left, then hard right. The road dead-ends in a few yards at a bar-be-que pit and shed. The house with brownish siding on the left is Aletha's. Usually open only on Thursdays, Fridays and Saturdays from about ten to ten, Miss Aletha stands on no formality. She runs the place with the help of children and grandchildren and there is not the first tainted hint of commercialism on the premise. There is the un-selfconscious ambience of visiting a friend and sitting around the kitchen table in another time. The dirt road across the railroad tracks seems to be a path to another era, a trail to a south Mississippi river bottom version of *Walton's Mountain*.

It's a short trip back over the tracks and the river to the realm of documented history. Columbia, a river port in the early 1800s, was briefly a capital of Mississippi. The legislatures of December 1821 and June 1822 met here.

But the most revered historic relic in the area is the John Ford House. Down Highway 35 South at Sandy Hook, you'll find another winding dirt road that will take you to the Ford House which local history buffs say was probably built sometime around 1810. Many people consider the Ford House to be the oldest surviving home in the Pearl River Valley. There are legends, myths and various versions of the "absolute" truth that

The Ford House, Sandy Hook, near Columbia.

will delight, entertain and puzzle you. You may want to draw your own lines between fact and fiction. The Pearl River Convention met here in 1816 and drew up a petition for statehood. Andrew Jackson slept here. Of course he got the best room in the house, but only after promising to put a check on his salty language. When danger lurked in the woods and swamps or on the river, settlers and honest folk huddled together in the stout house. The frontier appointments are still disarmingly pleasant.

The home is not always open on a regular basis. If you miss the signs for the house, you might stop at the Sandy Hook post office and ask directions. If the house is closed, you can still wander around the grounds and get a sense of the place.

Columbia is located on US 98 about 22 miles west of Hattiesburg.

Follow the signs down MS 35 south to Sandy Hook and the John Ford House, about 16 miles south of Columbia. In Sandy Hook turn left at the grocery store, follow the signs to the post office, go past the post office and take the first dirt road to the left. There are signs, which sometimes are hidden. If you cross a bridge without a railing you have passed the lane to the Ford house. Admission fee charged. Primitive restrooms. Telephone 601-736-4258.

To reach Aletha's—on US 98 West turn left at the state highway department building. Follow the frontage road back towards the river, take the first right—you'll see the railroad tracks to your left, then a left at the next road, then a hard right. Telephone 601-736-5163.

Some accommodations, restaurants and fast food establishments available in Columbia, others at Hattiesburg.

32
Hattiesburg

The New South's bold visions arrived in a little community along Gordon's Creek, near Kings' Ferry Crossing on the Leaf River, in the early 1880s when a self-styled entrepreneur came through the area plotting the course of a railroad.

That entrepreneur, William Hardy, is credited wtih founding a town virtually on the spot and naming it for his wife Hattie Lott in 1882–1884. The small community that already existed in the area is largely forgotten. But a mile or so from the sign in front of the old Federal Courthouse on Pine Street celebrating Hardy's founding of the town lies the homestead of one of the earliest white settlers in the region, a pioneer woman named Deliah Farrar who probably arrived in the 1820s. She made her "X" on the purchase agreement for Leaf River bottom land and President John Quincy Adams granted her patent. Other early white settlers' names have been given to outlying communities (Batson and Eatonville) or are only seen on the crumbling tablets of vine-ensnared graveyards.

Archaeologists have said the area of the pavilion in Kamper Park (along Gordon's Creek at Hardy Street) was once a camp site for pre-Columbian Indians. Over the years area residents have found numerous Stone Age tools and projectiles in the sandy soil. High points near the creek and river were also camp sites for various Native American bands over the ages. The Bouie (sometimes misspelled Bowie) River joins the Leaf at Hattiesburg (on US 11) and local legends claim that Indians believed such a fork in rivers was safe from tornadoes, and that the converging waters produced "good medicine."

The speed with which Hardy's railroad, coupled with the green-gold of the Piney Woods' great forests, rushed the new town into flush times may have seemed so much like magic, only "good medicine" could have created it. Some of the largest lumber mills in the country were in operation here. Workmen from the tiny communities and farms of the Piney Woods moved to the town. Some of the phenomenal wealth slashed from the forests lined the pockets of a few local timber barons and those who provided them services and merchandise, but for the most part the money migrated north. During the boom such migrations seemed to matter little. Prevailing wisdom suggested that if the timber ever ran out, if the river of money ever stopped flowing, the town would just take up some new industrial enterprises. Hattiesburg momentarily shared the optimism of the frontier as a progressive New South city without the scars of the Civil War or Reconstruction.

Then the timber was gone, the forest clear cut, the land eroded, the rivers and creeks silted up. The palatial hotels and establishments that had catered to the wealthy lumbermen, various entrepreneurs, bankers and railroad executives were empty. The businesses that had rushed to fulfill the needs and whims of the monied were idle. Hattiesburg had acquired a small degree of industrial/economic diversity, but not enough to support the city Hattiesburg's residents wanted. The cut-and-run philosophy of the New South exploiters left a bitter legacy.

Today Hattiesburg's historic downtown district, with its picture-perfect nostalgic storefront offices, is housed in the remnant of the posh, modern brick town built shortly after the turn of the century. (Previously fire had destroyed many of the original frame buildings in the district.) The streets are lined with crepe myrtles, rose gardens, ornamental pear trees and geranium patches. Oaks shade a whitewashed corner of the Forrest County Courthouse's space. The courthouse, the Masonic Temple, the Main Street Methodist Church and a fanciful Victorian home form an architectural quartet on Main Street that sings of a diversity of style. The Greek Revival inspired columns and grandeur of the temple and courthouse, the aged-red-brick church bell tower with its green-patina copper roof and the lacy wooden details of the McLeod House, now law offices, are a vision from the past. But the small, architecturally

A coed models a turn-of-the-century costume, from a collection of historic clothing owned by USM, against the backdrop of the McLeod House, Main Street, Hattiesburg.

inspiring downtown district composing only a few blocks is only a shadow of its former self.

A visitor from the past, a time traveler from 1910 or so, might imagine a horrendous war or killer cyclone had wiped away the burgeoning city that had emerged here around the turn of the century. Perhaps it was a type of war, a conflict of economic and cultural dimensions, that caused men to deliberately demolish most of the old town and move surviving businesses to sprawl-styled developments along the approaches to town.

Perhaps to understand the demolition one has to imagine it was caused not so much by a disrespect or an irreverence for history as a rejection of a bad memory. Perhaps it was a method of trying to forget how economic invaders plundered the land and exploited the people.

Only in recent years have the city fathers moved to stop further loss of architectural treasures. In the early 1980s Mayor Bobby Chain pioneered Hattiesburg's downtown historic restoration projects. This was a momentous occasion in the life of a town that has the potential to become a featured stop for visitors yearning for an interlude among structures of the Victorian-Edwardian eras.

Today the legacies of the mammoth lumber company operators who ruled Hattiesburg's economy are few. Basically all they left is a few Victorian era homes ("pine palaces") of company officials. The last several blocks of Buschman and Newman Streets, which now end in a cul-de-sac, were once the J.J. Newman Lumber Company compound containing the company's headquarters and the homes of some officials. Millhands lived across Gordon's Creek from the compound in a largely abandoned area still called the Newman Quarters. The compound had its own electricity, telephone and fire protection systems. Many people say the Newman lumber company was once the largest in the world. Hattiesburg was a star division in its vast holdings. Local historians claim that for several years during the boom time, J.J. Newman at Hattiesburg led the world in number of board feet of lumber shipped.

Main Street, the downtown artery, ends at the intersection

with Buschman Street. What appears to be a continuation of Main Street is the beginning of Bay Street. Today the Bay Street area is a potpourri of Victorian, Queen Anne, Edwardian and more modern architectural styles that would delight a Hollywood set designer. The Turner House, circa 1904, 500 Bay Street, is open to the public as a museum to the lifestyles and interests of Hattiesburg's more affluent citizens during the days of the timber barons.

Back down Main Street, Mrs. Curry's boarding house, an establishment with no signs and no advertising, is a thriving business carry-over from turn-of-the-century traditions. At 923 North Main Street, the boarding house caters to the needs of another era with such detail that it has appeared in various television specials and movies. Lunch, usually a set menu of fried chicken daily and various casseroles and rich desserts on Sundays, is available to guests and the public for a modest fee.

The University of Southern Mississippi has catered to the educational needs of several generations of Mississippians since its founding in 1912. Hattiesburg's most notable landmark, at the corner of US 49 and US 98, the school is the home of the John Martin Frazier Museum of Natural Science. The museum's growing collection of antique Choctaw baskets details the methods, materials and traditions of the native Mississippian art form. Also tucked away in a secluded university courtyard (Psychology Department Building) is an authentic one-room schoolhouse rescued from the Piney Woods by a benefactor. Not yet listed for organized tours, the school can be viewed by visitors simply going to the psychology building's courtyard.

Native forests hug the outer limits of the city on all sides. Heading south on US 11, just before the land is swallowed up by pines, a historic marker is placed near the spot, Richburg Hill, where John Sullivan and Jake Kilrain slugged their way through 75 rounds of an illegal bareknuckled fight sponsored by New Orleans sports promoters. Sports fans still get excited when they talk of how after this particular style of fighting had been outlawed in 1889, a Hattiesburg man visiting New Orleans happened to mention a natural amphitheater in the deep woods near his home that would be a perfect setting for the forbidden bout. When word got out that there would be a fight, legends claim, the governor of Mississippi called out the militia and put guards on all the main roads coming into Mississippi as well as having the militia watch all incoming trains. But the promoters cleverly snuck the fighters into the wilderness and sold tickets for $10 apiece to a great number of fans. Allegedly law enforcement officials were able to arrest the fighters and promoters only after the fight. (They were fined.) Sullivan won the fight, which is remembered as the last bare-knuckle championship bout in the U.S.A.

The highway quickly runs by the marker, heading into the wilderness nature and reforestation has created.

Hattiesburg is located at the junction of US 98 and US 49 on I-59 about 69 miles north of Gulfport and 88 south of Jackson.

For a free brochure of a self-guided driving tour of Hattiesburg Historic Neighborhood District, an area of about 115 acres of homes built between 1880 and 1930 near the downtown district, contact Historic Driving Tour, c/o Historic Neighborhood, 515 Walnut Street, Hattiesburg, MS 39401. Telephone 601-545-7620.

Turner House, 500 Bay Street, is open for tours by appointment. Telephone 601-582-1771. Admission free.

Frazier Natural Science Museum operates on a schedule that is geared to the university's academic calendar. Telephone 601-266-4747. Admission free.

Mrs. Curry's, located at 923 North Main Street appears to be a prosperous private home. If you are coming for lunch, walk around the house to the back entrance. There are no signs. Telephone 601-545-1100.

33
Lucedale—Palestinian Gardens

The best place to learn the history of the Bible is on the road between Jericho and Jerusalem in Palestine according to Harvell Jackson. Born in the early years of this century, Jackson became so convinced that geography was the key to better understanding biblical history, that he began to dream of building a Palestine in miniature soon after he left the seminary and began his ministry.

Today his replica Holy Land is a reality. Surrounded by lush vegetation and sheltered by tall pines, the scale model is called Palestinain Gardens. Rev. Jackson, a Presbyterian minister, and his wife Pelleree have recreated Palestine as it was in biblical days on 20 acres of woodland 12 miles north of Lucedale. The scale in relation to the Holy Land is about one yard per mile.

Mrs. Jackson became a partner in the dream of building the miniature Holy Land when she married the preacher. Jackson dedicated his ministry to country churches, and as they traveled about the south, serving small rural churches, they worked on their plans. They lived off of the preacher's small salary and Mrs. Jackson went to work as a schoolteacher. Her salary was saved for the dream.

After about 18 years the Jacksons found what they thought to be the perfect piece of land in south Mississippi, bought it and began building. Jackson says the lay of the land on their particular site is so close to a scaled down version of the Holy Land's topography that "Only God could have led us here."

The houses in the miniature biblical cities were built by hand. Concrete blocks and plaster were the main construction materials. Several of the domed buildings were made from automobile headlights, attached to concrete blocks and covered

*Harvell Jackson created a scale model Holy Land in his Palestinian
Gardens, Lucedale.*

with plaster. The Jacksons did all the work themselves and
learned how to turn the blocks into facsimiles of houses by trial
and error.

The couple bought the property for their miniature Holy
Land in 1954. Working after school and when there were lulls
in pastoral duties, they were able to open the gardens in 1960.

The gardens have a rustic and naturally peaceful atmosphere.
The Jacksons landscaped the biblical setting with azaleas, dogwoods and camellias. In the spring the gardens explode with
flowers and color. From the Jordan Valley to the Jericho Road,
from Bethlehem to Jerusalem, from Ephraim to Nazareth to the
Sea of Galilee, guides recall the men and women who laid the
foundation for the Christian religions as well as the historical
events that shaped those foundations.

Though the Jacksons are Presbyterian, Palestinian Gardens is
a non-profit corporation and is not sponsored by any church or
group.

Palestinian Gardens, located off of US 98, has signs on the southeastern side of the Chickasawhay River bridge in George County that point to a country road trail that leads over 6.5 miles to the gardens. The gardens are open March through November from 8 a.m. to 4 p.m. each day. There are picnic facilities and restrooms on the grounds. Address: Palestinian Gardens, Route 9, Box 792, Lucedale, MS 39452. Telephone 601-947-8422. Admission fee charged.

Accommodations, restaurants and fast food establishments are located in Lucedale along US 98 about 60 miles southeast of Hattiesburg.

34

The Coast—Bay St. Louis, Pass Christain, Gulfport, and Biloxi

Mississippi's southern coastline communities are a world away from the rest of the state philosophically. History binds the string of waterfront towns together, if not in a common heritage, at least in a similar heritage that further separates coastal attitudes from those found inland.

A carefree lifestyle that doesn't exist in other parts of the state dictates the rhythm of activities here. Sometimes the attitude of the people is attributed to a French influence, but an old Biloxi Indian legend suggests a different reason. The legend foretold the coming of white people as a homecoming. The Indians claimed that the white people had lived on the coast in another age and would eventually return, because to find contentment here people just had to eat the fish and oysters and drink from the local springs.

This basic philosophy of carefree contentment easily found has dovetailed with the resort and tourist businesses which have been a major industry on the coast since the early 1800s. Starting at Clermont Harbor west of Bay St. Louis, visitors can wind through the stages of coast history in a self-guided driving tour.

You can reach Clermont Harbor, at the far west end of Waveland, from US 90 by choosing one of the southbound streets bordered by wind-sculpted live oaks and Victorian-styled seaside cottages which squeeze closer and closer together as the beach nears. But the beach front still has small stretches of undeveloped pine woods and grasslands. The drive from the harbor passes a gallery of both modern and historic beach homes. Though hurricanes have swept many away over the years, there are enough left to give an idea of the refuge from the heat offered by these long, low houses with their expanses of porches facing seaward.

There's always been a magic at the sea's edge, an allure of wind and mist, rushing tides and gull songs that sooth the soul. Yesterday's and today's moments of inner peace merge as smoothly as the shadowy ships in the distance slip into the haze. According to legends pirates and adventurers seeking a different sort of peace, a respite from the long reaches of the prevailing law found a haven at Waveland. Hurricane Camille, 1969, swept away the Blake House which was locally known as the Pirate's house. In 1802 the "overlord" of the gulf coast pirates, calling himself a "New Orleans businessman" built a comfortable and casually elegant Louisiana style planter's home here. Supposedly there was a secret tunnel from the house to the waterfront. According to legend this chief pirate was Jean Lafitte's boss and rallied the Batarians and his other cohorts into the ranks of Andrew Jackson's forces at the Battle of New Orleans.

Without signs you might never know where Waveland ends and Bay St. Louis begins. Bay St. Louis was called Chicapoula by the Indians. Jean Baptiste Le Moyne Bienville named the area for the bay his brother d'Iberville had named in honor of a sainted King of France (Louis IX). John Law, of the Mississippi Bubble land-fraud scheme, gave the land around the bay to a Madame de Mezieres in 1720; then about 1789 the Spaniards gave Thomas Shields a land grant for the area and for a while the town was called Shieldsborough. For the most part the area was settled by French-Canadians who intermarried with local Indians and displayed a particular disdain for governments.

Bay St. Louis was the scene of the "Battle of Pass Christian" in 1814 when a ragtag little American flotilla of five gunboats sought refuge in the shallow waters of the bay after tweaking the tail of the British lion (a fleet of about 60 warships) as it passed on its way to the Battle of New Orleans. The Americans thought they'd be safe in the bay because the big British ships couldn't follow in the shallow water. But heavily armed small boats and launches put out from the fleet and within a very short time, legends say less than an hour, all the American gunboats were captured or sunk.

At the time of the battle the town was already a popular summer retreat for wealthy planters. The local permanent population's strong Catholic heritage is reflected in historic churches and schools such as St. Stanislaus College (1854). A legacy of beachfront cottages intermingle with businesses along Beach Boulevard as it winds its way back to US 90.

Across the bay at Pass Christian, named for the discoverer of the "pass" old maps show running between the mainland and the barrier islands, the U.S. Army stationed a garrison in 1811. As planters and businessmen from Mississippi, Alabama and Louisiana established vacation homes on the coast, a contingent of officers and men of the Mounted Regiment of Creek Indian Volunteers ordered into militia service of the U.S. prior to September 1837 were stationed here. The muster rolls of September 1837 show that some of the men brought their families and that others died while here.

By the 1880s northern tourists started spending the winter here, and in 1913 President Woodrow Wilson came for a stay, and the home he visited was declared the "Dixie White House." Supposedly President Wilson frequently visited the Town Library, a white frame building tucked under the trees up the embankment from the small boat harbor. A historic signpost marks the vicinity of the Dixie White House on Beach Boulevard.

A 26-mile-long man-made beach begins at Pass Christian and stretches to the Biloxi-Ocean Springs Bridge. Beach Boulevard, US 90, hugs the coastline as it winds into the next coast town, Long Beach. Legends claim that the town was once the site of an Indian village. At the University of Southern Mississippi's Gulf Park Campus, a 500-year-old live oak, called the Friendship Oak, once sheltered the classes of poet Vachel Linsay in its limbs.

The beach gives way to Gulfport's banana boat terminals, said to be the largest in the world. Gulfport, an outgrowth of the state's timber and railroad boom, came into being in the late

The Magnolia Hotel, Biloxi, was a pioneer establishment in the Gulf Coast's resort industry.

1880s. After a brief commercial interruption the beach stretches out again, arching its sandy back against the seawall reaching towards Biloxi. Grass Lawn, 720 East Beach, is a Gulfport landmark older than Gulfport. This summer home, circa 1836, with its wide galleries, is typical of early vacation homes built on the coast so the wealthy could escape the heat and the fevers of the cities and inland plantations.

In Biloxi, Beauvoir, Jefferson Davis's last home, faces the beach with its summer population of sun and water worshippers. The next landmark down the beach, the Biloxi Lighthouse, has been sending out its guiding beam for 13 miles since 1848. The lighthouse, a cast-iron structure 65-feet tall, has a long history of women keepers. An exhibit in the base of the lighthouse explores the structures' history.

Different lifestyles are explored at three Biloxi sites, the Magnolia Hotel, The Old Brick House and the Tullis-Toledano manor. The Magnolia Hotel, circa 1847, an antebellum survivor of the town's pre-Civil War resort clientele is now an art gallery and museum within the Vieux Marche downtown area.

The Old Brick House, circa 1790, 410 East Bayview Avenue, one of the oldest surviving buildings in Biloxi, is today in a neighborhood of boatyards, small docks and fishermen's homes.

The Tullis-Toledano Manor, circa 1856, is a restored beach-front home featuring double galleries, original furnishings and displays of area architectural history. The red brick house under expansive spreading oaks looks toward Deer Island just a short distance across the water.

The present site of Biloxi became the seat of government for French Louisiana about 1719 until the capital moved to New Orleans around 1722. The early population here mirrored the early population patterns of Bay St. Louis. Primarily French-Canadians and French military men, the first settlers preferred to marry local Indian women, rather than the potential brides the French government sent over with small cases (*casettes*) containing state provided "marriage outfits."

Biloxi, the best known and most popular of the Gulf Coast resort towns, was a stop on the steamboat route from New Orleans to Mobile in 1827. Though a contingent of local men

Tullis-Toledano Manor, now a museum, is a neighbor to the seafood industries and Seafood Museum, Biloxi.

formed the Confederate Biloxi Rifles during the Civil War, and Biloxi suffered through a Union blockade with little more to sustain life than "Biloxi-bacon" (mullett), the events of the war within the city are largely uncelebrated. Soon after the war Biloxi resumed its position as a "watering place" of choice for the affluent, and with the coming of the railroads in the 1870s, the town's seafood industry boomed. New waves of immigrants arrived from southeastern Europe, especially Yugoslavia, and meshed their customs and traditions into the tapestry of Biloxi lifestyles, scarcely causing a ripple in the community's ongoing contentment.

The pattern continues today. The latest wave of immigrants meshing their customs and traditions into the local tapestry are

Vietnamese. Contentment, even for visitors, is only as far away as a seafood dinner at any one of dozens of good restaurants or maybe a "po'boy" sandwich at some fisherman's neighborhood haunt such as the Biloxi Schooner on East Howard Avenue.

From US 90 at Waveland turn south, go to land's end and follow Beach Boulevard west to Clermont Harbor, where the highway ends, come back along the beach through Bay St. Louis to US 90 and the bridge to Pass Christain. For an easy tour of the coast follow US 90 to the Ocean Springs bridge at Biloxi.

For information about any Gulf Coast attractions, contact the Gulf Coast Convention and Visitors Bureau by telephone 601-388-8000 or 800-237-9493.

Grass Lawn, Box 651, Gulfport, MS 39502. Telephone 601-864-5019. Admission fee charged.

Biloxi Light House, c/o City Parks, Recreation & Cultural Affairs Department, Box 775, Biloxi, MS 39533. Telephone 601-435-6294. Admission fee charged.

Magnolia Hotel, Box 667, Biloxi, MS 39533. Telephone 601-432-5682. Admission free.

Old Brick House, 410 East Bayview Avenue, Biloxi, MS 39530. Telephone 601-432-0336. Admission fee charged.

Tullis-Toledano Manor, Box 775, Biloxi, MS 39533. Telephone 601-435-6294. Admission free.

The Biloxi Schooner is a neighborhood restaurant catering to locals, fishermen and shrimpers—an outpost of "how it use to be" without any pretentious trappings. Po'boys, sandwiches on French bread, are still as good as they "use to be" here. Located at the corner of East Howard and Myrtle Street at the foot of the old Biloxi Bridge. Telephone 601-374-8071.

Accommodations, restaurants and fast food establishments are plentiful all along the coast. The "season" is usually considered to run from April to September. Motels and hotels offer reduced rates out of season.

35
Biloxi—Beauvoir

Hundreds of ghostly Confederate spirits populate Beauvoir's nights. Behind the high broad fences that guard Jefferson Davis' antebellum home here, rebel spirits roam the shadowy grounds, policing haunted memories. Most anyone who has ever spent the night here testifies that he has felt their presence, known they were about the place.

These spirits of men who wore grey did not come here as the proud and mighty, even though they once may have been bold and obliging warriors. These men, about 700 in all, were the elderly and ill, defeated by the universal enemies of man, time and aging.

In the front vestibule of the main house, the ticket punching hostess marks her place in the romance novel she reads between visitors and explains, "They were without family, old, sick and destitute. If they had had family, they wouldn't have come here. Their families would have taken them in."

Usually there is someone about who will explain how Mrs. Jefferson Davis sold the president of the Confederacy's last home to the Mississippi Sons of the Confederacy organization in 1902 for $10,000 with the stipulation that it be used as a home for veterans, their wives and widows. The original document also called for the home to take in any Confederate veterans' orphans and ex-slaves who might need a home. In 1904 when the state of Mississippi took over the management of Beauvoir as a home for Confederate veterans, their wives and widows, the legislature deleted Mrs. Davis' inclusion of orphans and slaves.

By 1940 the need for the "old soldiers" home had lessened so much that the Mississippi Division of the Sons of Confederate

Beauvoir, Jefferson Davis' last home, Biloxi.

Veterans had a bill passed in the state legislature to convert Beauvoir into a Jefferson Davis Shrine. The last Confederate widows were moved from Beauvoir to a nursing home in 1951.

There's no denying there is a hushed reverence about the place. The sort of quiet and peace you'd expect to find in a shrine. Sometimes in the world beyond Beauvoir's walls, there is a smirk when the uninitiated speak of the "Shrine." Practitioners of automatic assumptions may be laboring under an illusion that this is the last realm of the lost cause, the burying ground of ideals that cannons and swords could not impose or enforce.

Inside the old hospital, now the Confederate Museum, there is a glimmer of that—tattered battle flags, moth eaten uniforms, murals of the cause's champions, but there is too much detail for the discerning visitor to translate into such a simple text.

There are the Indian artifacts, arrowheads, tools and bits of earth molded into vessels, along with the fine china of a grand house, a chapel, pulpit and pews, and the surgical implements of southern physicians—all of which tend to speak to a broader issue.

The pavilion where Jefferson Davis wrote his major works (*The Rise and Fall of the Confederate Government* and *A Short History of the Confederate States*) with its wide, tall glass panelled doors looking out on the sea, the broad wide welcoming hallway of the main house, his modest, near spartan, bedroom do conjure up memories we sometimes can only daydream into reality.

This is a place you want to come home to, a place you want to come to visit with an elderly relative. A Biloxi native, in his mid-50s, shares his earliest memories of visiting Beauvoir. He came here often in the late '30s and early '40s to visit an ancient female relative who had sought the shrine's refuge. His memories of the barracks accommodations and main house are fuzzy. But the visits themselves retain bold proportions because the revered relative had a parrot. On a wrought-iron bench, under a shade tree, your hair tousled by the Gulf breeze, you can close your eyes and see the Biloxi native's ancient relative, a parrot on her shoulder, coming out of the haze, moving towards you.

Here at Beauvoir you can go back in time to places half-remembered from childhood, if you had a southern childhood, back to where you could still glimpse the sweet order of a lifestyle that was fading fast even then. The green lattice on the back veranda filters the light and softens the harsh glare of the modern world. It's safe here, safe to wander backward through the dimmed light and peek in on a family's memories. The dining room, butler's pantry and children's dining room line one side of the veranda. Jefferson Davis' bedroom is on the other. Mrs. Davis' bedroom adjoins her husband's.

Downstairs the basement offers all the ambience of your favorite aunt's family attic. Family treasures are everywhere—locks of hair, a beloved daughter's sketchbooks, scrapbooks, letters, a favorite dress, and pressed flowers. There are other more historic mementoes here, too, even a carriage, but the personal memorabilia let you imagine that you are establishing a intimate link with a loving, devoted family.

Inside the old hospital there is a souvenir and gift shop with special southern oriented merchandise, including a selection of books.

Besides the house, pavilions and museums, the grounds contain paths, trails and walks for leisurely strolling, and a replica of the barracks where the old soldiers lived; a lagoon with a foot bridge leads to a cemetery where Jefferson Davis' father is buried and the tomb of the unknown soldier of the Confederate States of America is located.

If you are interested in learning more about the former owner, a man who was once a West Point Cadet, frontier soldier, planter, member of U.S. House of Representatives, Mexican War general, U.S. senator, U.S. Secretary of War, as well as President of the Confederate States of America, you will find Hudson Strode's multi-volume biography of Jefferson Davis informative and enlightening.

Beauvoir, located on the beach on US 90, Biloxi, east of the Coliseum, is open daily from 8:30 a.m. till 5 p.m. Admission fee charged. Telephone 601-388-1313.

Accommodations, restaurants and fast food establishments are plentiful in Biloxi.

36
Biloxi—Seafood Museum

A tribute to people "wed to the water" is how Biloxi Mayor
Gerald Blessey described the Seafood Industry Museum when it
opened in 1986. Located in a Spanish-styled building that once
was a Coast Guard barracks at the foot of the Biloxi-Ocean
Springs Bridge, the museum celebrates Biloxi's economic
heritage while allowing visitors to explore the working world of
local people who've earned their livelihoods from oystering,
shrimping and fishing.

The tour of the museum begins with maps of the ancient gulf
coastline and quickly moves to depictions of the Taneksanya,
the early Biloxi Indians, and their unique settlements guarded
by watch towers. Indian artifacts found along the coast are
displayed. The distant origins of some items demonstrate that
these early people were involved in trade from many areas.
Other pieces show local oyster shells were cooked down and
used for pottery. Fragments of pottery and an Indian oyster
knife are on display. According to legends the Indians went
oystering with their bare hands.

When the French arrived in the early colonial period, they
noted the abundance of seafood and left records of wading out
at low tide and picking up fish with their bare hands.

Then there's the story of a U.S. government official arriving
from New Orleans about 1811 and finding a community of
Frenchmen and French-Indian mixed bloods where no one
could read or write English.

Advertisements from New Orleans newspapers a few years
later attempted to entice vacationers to Biloxi, and apparently
they were successful. A number of hotels sprung up in the area.
One Biloxi hotel's advertisement claimed its own crew of

oystermen and fishermen to provide fresh seafood daily for its restaurant.

There are bits and pieces of burned packet boats, a lens from the Ship Island lighthouse; telegrams and notes telling a twisted tale of how during the Civil War fishermen from Biloxi were put in an Confederate infantry unit and sent to Kentucky. Photographs highlight lists of canneries in different years. The canneries' name document area family names.

Nets hang from the ceiling and there is a brief course, mounted on the wall, in how to throw a net in a few easy steps. The boats of Biloxi are detailed from the "launches" of the first French colonists, to the cat boat, the Biloxi Cat, the New Orleans Lugger, and the Biloxi Schooner. Most surviving boats of these types and related artifacts were collected by the Smithsonian Institution in the 1930s and removed from the area.

Everywhere there are the tools of the trades and photographs documenting men and families at work. Plans are eventually to have actual working boats on display and audio recordings of actual fishermen working on the boats playing for visitors as they look at the exhibits.

Biloxi's architectural heritage is featured in a separate exhibit called "The houses that seafood built." Often the more grandiose structures were swept away by hurricanes. Many of the simple cottages have survived.

The most poignant exhibit in the museum is the collection of photos from the Child Labor Report to the U.S. Congress from the early years of this century. Photographer Lewis Hine captured images of children working alongside adults, or with their own families in times when an entire family had to pull together just to survive.

Throughout the museum visitors can easily see the social and cultural history of Biloxi has been unique and enduring. The people have never lost touch with elements of their heritage. Perhaps the most intriguing element of the museum for a non-Biloxi native is there has been no attempt to embellish the memory of a working people's past. The exhibits are refreshing in their honesty.

The Seafood Museum is located just off US 90 at the foot of the Biloxi-Ocean Springs Bridge. Address: Seafood Industry Museum, Inc., P.O. Box 1907, Biloxi, Mississippi, 39533. Telephone 601-435-6320. Open Monday through Saturday 9 a.m. to 5 p.m. Admission fee charged.

Accommodations, restaurants and fast food establishments are plentiful in Biloxi.

Seafood Museum, Biloxi.

37
Ocean Springs

Washington Avenue runs out to US 90, alluring and enticing with its massive oaks creating a tunnel of shade for sun-weary travelers, offering an escape route to the unhurried, relaxed lifestyle of a seaside community. The old depot that serves as the Chamber of Commerce Building and an art gallery, stands sentinel at the corner of the highway and the avenue.

Ocean Springs has been offering a retreat, a respite for veterans of the world's ills and woes for well over a century. In the early 1850s a New Orleans physician established a sanitarium here to take advantage of spring waters the Indians had long considered medicinal. A spa was born. Shortly thereafter villagers adopted the doctor's suggested name for the village, Ocean Springs. Up until then, the community, which officially called itself Lynchburg, had most often been known as "old Biloxi."

The Community Center, just a short distance from the US 90 and Washington Avenue intersection, tells the story of the arrival of the first European colonists in graphic style. The murals on the center's inside walls were painted by Ocean Springs' most famous artist, Walter Anderson. A philosopher and poet as well as painter, early in his career Anderson wrote in his journal that an artist has an obligation to the community to create objects of beauty that are both useful and affordable. He worked on the murals for about a year and a half in the early 1950s. His fee was $1. In the early 1980s they were valued at $1 million. In painted visions Pierre le Moyne d'Iberville and his band of French adventurers claim the land for France. Capturing the essence and nuances of the historic 1699 moment in line, form and color, the artist's imagination becomes a magic transport, a way for viewers not only to see the event, but feel its magnitude—from the grit of sand underfoot, to the slick polished wood of the staff holding the silk Fleur de lis, to the sheltering barrier of pines in the distance.

Just a few blocks away on Beach Drive, a street that hugs the shoreline from the foot of the Biloxi-Ocean Springs Bridge to the Ocean Springs Harbor, a re-created primitive Fort Maurepas stands near the site of the first French fort on a curve between Fort Bayou and Davis Bayou. Legends claim this site was favored because it faced both the Mississippi Sound and the Gulf of Mexico.

Lacking pragmatic skills essential for survival in their new environment, the Frenchmen became dependent on the local Indians. They adopted the tribe's name, Biloxi, for their settlement. Biloxi was the seat of government for all the land France claimed within the watershed drained by the Mississippi River until 1702 when the government moved to Mobile. The government returned about 1719, then moved itself and Biloxi across the bay to that city's present location shortly thereafter.

Fort Maurepas (re-created), Ocean Springs.

Old Biloxi became an Indian trading post. As late as 1852 residents had to sail across the bay to New Biloxi for their mail.

But with the opening of the early health spa, the small settlement became a popular resort and the steamboat line that operated between New Orleans and Mobile started making regular stops. Over the years many New Orleans' residents bought summer homes at Ocean Springs, among them were Walter Anderson's parents.

Their retreat, Shearwater, named for a type of gull, reflects the history of the area as a place of summer homes as well as the retreat and refuge of creative souls. A magic tangle of coastal wilderness, painstakingly unmanicured, beside the harbor, Shearwater is open to the public.

Here Walter's brother Peter founded and operated the Shearwater Pottery, and Walter's mother built a showroom for her sons' work. The three Anderson sons (Walter, Peter and Mac) became artists and all three made their homes within the 25-acre Shearwater compound. Peter's son James is carrying on his father's work and several younger members of the family are pursuing artistic endeavors. The pottery, workshop and showroom are staffed by family. The showroom, jutting out into the wild woods, gives visitors the perspective of being inside an oriental landscape. As artistically and stylistically unique as Walter's paintings, it has the ambience and quiet charm of a private museum. Works by the three sons, as well as pieces from the succeeding generations are on display.

One day a week Walter's house is also open for tours. The house's origins are humble. A two-room servant's cottage, Walter transformed the place into a world of light and color. On the screened-in front porch, an iron bedstead fills one end while the opposite side shelters the wooden Greek ship Ulysses sailed through Walter's tales from the Odyssey, which he not only read, but acted out for his children. The cottage is stuffed with his works—from carved linoleum blocks to hand-carved furniture. Few walls escaped the artist's brush. Even the bathroom has its murals. But the masterpiece of the house is what is now called the "mural room." Kept locked and private during his lifetime, not even family members saw the room until after his death in 1965. You enter the room as you would the first day of spring. The joy of creation is overpowering. The color, the wonder, the resurgence of life grips the vital line between heart and eyes. The mural depicts a day on the coast— a day populated by birds and flowers, insects and plants, animals and color. Even the ceiling unfolds the petal of a chrysanthemum opening to infinity.

Anderson's skiff is tucked under the edge of the house as if it might be pulled out at any moment to ferry the artist the 13 miles across the sound to Horn Island. The island was his favorite subject during his last years.

The natural wonders of the area that conspired to seduce the artistic talents of the Andersons have also worked their spell on other artists. Ocean Springs is now often spoke of as a community of artists.

A day, almost any time of year, in Ocean Springs—driving along the oak shaded streets, meandering along the shoreline watching the wind surfers and sail boats glide across the water with Deer Island's pines in the background—is an example of nature's own art.

Oceans Springs is located on US 90 across the bay from Biloxi. Accommodations, restaurants and fast food establishments are available.

Community Center, 514 Washington Avenue. Telephone 601-875-8833. Open by appointment. Admission free.

Shearwater Pottery, from US 90 take Washington Avenue to Government Street, left on Government to Pershing, Right on Pershing to Shearwater. There are signs along the way. Telephone 601-875-7320. Pottery workshop open Monday through Friday 9 a.m. to 4 p.m. Showroom open everyday. Walter Anderson cottage open one day a week, usually Thursday, best to call in advance to see cottage. Admission free.

38
Pascagoula—The Singing River

The Pascagoula River sings its song, whispering of the past in ancient language and prehistoric rhythms. The song never ceases, but in late summer or early autumn when the sultry breezes carry slight promises of cooler days, the music grows louder and more distinct.

The mysterious music sounds like "buzzing bees" to some listeners. Other listeners captivated by the magic of the singing river hear a more romantic sound. William Baxter, after a 1848 visit wrote, "This music is generally heard about nightfall when it strikes upon the ear like the breathing of an Aeolian harp in the distance; scarcely, however has a feeling of delight been awakened by the distant strain when wonder is excited by the seeming approach of this fairylike music. A moment before, and the ear could only catch a faint, distant, dying cadence, now it swells louder, becomes more and more distinct, until it seems within a few feet of where you stand. It is then, truly mysterious, for though sensible that it is near you, you are totally unable to locate the sound, but it seems to issue from any point to which you direct your attention. It is in the above, below, and all around when you listen, thence the music seems to flow."

The song is so timeless we can stand on the river banks today and hear the music as clearly and precisely as Baxter described it. Scientists offer several possible theories for the phenomenon. The song may be made by a type of fish, the grating of sand on the river's slate bottom, a current being sucked past a hidden cave, or natural gas escaping from the sand beds. Those who can hear Aeolian harps and fairylike music enjoy imagining that there are other causes for the river's song.

The most enduring legend explaining the river's song tells how a gentle but proud tribe of ancient Americans were attacked by hostile neighbors while their warrior/hunters were away. Rather than face the humiliation of surrender and sub-jugation, the old men, women and children walked into the river chanting their death songs and drowned themselves, giving their souls to the water. The legend says it is their death chant the river sings.

A variation on this story has been adopted by the city of Pascagoula as the "official" legend of the Singing River. The official story romantically tells of how a young princess of the Biloxi tribe, though betrothed to a chieftain of her own war-like people, fell in love with a young chieftain of the peace-loving Pascagoula tribe and ran off with him. The jilted Biloxi chief-tain led a band of warriors in an attack on the Pascagoula. Though the Pascagoula chieftain offered to turn himself over to the Biloxis in atonement after the attack was underway, his people said no. The Pascagoula swore they'd either save the young couple or die with them. When the Biloxis' victory was near, the Pascagoula sent their women and children into the river to drown; the warriors then joined hands, and chanting their death song followed them.

Much of the town of Pascagoula's history is cocooned in the same sort of romantic legends as the Singing River's. If you peel away too many layers of the carefully spun capsules, you may destroy the entities, the historic facts they shelter. Pascagoula means bread eater or bread maker or bread people. The Pas-cagoula Indians who lived here when the first French explorers arrived were peaceful, friendly and helpful. According to ar-chaeologists the number of Native American sites in the modern town, especially in the vicinity of the waterfront is phenomenal. Evidence suggests habitations here as far back as 1600 years. One skeleton of a young Indian man found has been dated at approximately 650 years old.

When d'Iberville established his Biloxi colony at Ocean Springs in 1699, he also explored the Pascagoula area. Accord-ing to local stories, upon his arrival he was "cordially" greeted by the Pascagoula Indians, which included the descendants of a small band of Acadians who arrived in the area in 1634, and a small tribe known as the Moctobi.

A youngster in d'Iberville's crew, 12-year-old Joseph Simon de la Pointe, became the master of Pascagoula a few years later. De la Pointe's kinswoman, Mme. de Chaumont, who has been variously described as "a woman of fortune," a lady-in-waiting to Princess Henrietta at the Fountainbleau court, and a mistress of Louis XIV, received a grant for the area. Some local historians say the grant was registered in Paris in 1711, others say it was a grant made in the Mississippi Bubble days of John Law around 1718. De la Pointe came into possession of the town site and built an estate. A carpenter shop, circa 1721, on his estate grounds survives as the Old Spanish Fort.

Considered by many to be the oldest standing structure in the Mississippi valley, Old Spanish Fort has a cosmopolitan background. The 300 settlers de la Pointe brought to establish his colony were German and eventually his daughter Marie married a German immigrant, Hugo Krebs. The couple made their home in the old carpenter shop. A granddaughter of the Krebs married a Spanish army officer when the area was under Spanish dominion and at that time the newlyweds decided to make their home in the old carpenter shop and fortified the premises. The Old Spanish Fort became a landmark on Krebs Lake, one of the numerous small lakes and bayous around the mouth of the Pascagoula River.

Though additions made to the original structure have come and gone, the original building is contained within the present middle room of the three surviving rooms. Walls are covered with a ground oyster shell plaster with *bousillage* (a mixture of clay and moss) underneath. Fireplaces are at both ends of the middle room and in each end room, hearths are elevated several feet, stout wooden-grooved ceiling beams are exposed and the building is encircled with a porch. A nearby cemetery contains generations of the Krebs family.

Guns from British warships captured during the War of 1812 decorate the grounds. A small museum on the grounds houses a mixture of pre-Columbian artifacts, memorabilia from the early 1800s and the Civil War period.

Old Spanish Fort, Pascagoula.

Across town the Longfellow House looks across the water to Ingalls West Bank shipbuilding facility. Perhaps this is a modern version of the view that inspired the poet Henry Wadsworth Longfellow to write "The Building of the Ship" on "Pascagoula's sunny bay." The poet visited the home shortly after it was built in the 1850s. Called Bellvue in those days, the house knew a variety of owners from the New Orleans slave trader who built it to an owner who rented it out for a girls' school (the girls scratched their names in the glass of an upper-story windowpane) to the present owners who use it as a headquarters for a waterfront restaurant and resort.

On the far western side of the river, in and around the town and waters of Gautier, David Glasgow Farragut, a native of Tennessee, spent boyhood days with his adopted family. He turned his knowledge of local waters to the Union's advantage during the Civil War, capturing the city of New Orleans and then, damning the torpedos and steaming full speed ahead, captured Mobile by sailing into the bay under the Confederate guns at Fort Morgan. The boy who played at the edge of the Pascagoula became the first admiral in the U.S. Navy.

Stopping at the rest and welcome stations along I-10, visitors can walk along the banks of the Pascagoula, listen for the song in the wild wood groves bordering the river and be pulled into a near hypnotic trance that make all the stories to be heard here very believable.

Pascagoula, located on US 90, at I-10 approximately 20 miles east of Biloxi, is just a few miles from the Alabama border. Accommodations available. Wide variety of fast food establishments and restaurants.

Old Spanish Fort, 4602 Fort Drive, Pascagoula, MS 39567. Telephone 601-769-1505. Open year round. Schedule changes, call first. Admission fee charged.

Longfellow House, a restaurant and resort, is located at 3401 Beach Boulevard, Pascagoula, MS 39567. Telephone 601-762-1122.

Write the Jackson County Area Chamber of Commerce, P.O. Drawer P, 825 US 90, Pascagoula, MS 39567 for information or write or call the Jackson County Welcome Center, I-10, P.O. Box 5181, Kreole Station, Moss Point, MS 39563. Telephone 601-475-3384.

39
Ship Island

The *Pan American Clipper* slices through the thick summer haze, leaving Biloxi behind as she heads out across the Mississippi Sound for Ship Island, one of the Barrier Islands that separate the shallow sound from the deep water of the Gulf of Mexico. By the time the brown water of the sound is tinged with a hint of clear green, Biloxi is a tree-topped fringe rising above a thin white strip of sand beach.

The *Clipper's* passengers face southward, watching for land, entertained by dolphins frolicking in the spray at the boat's bow, mellowed by the magic elixir of sea air. It's a dreamy journey, about one and a half hours, across the 12-mile stretch of the sound. There is time to imagine how the world must have looked on the other side of the island, the Gulf side, when the French explorer Pierre le Moyne d'Iberville dropped anchor in the island's deep water harbor back in 1699.

Through the haze shrimp boats trawling the sound become almost as ghostly and shadowy as history's memory of the billowing white canvas sails and stout wooden bows of the French explorers' ships.

The *Clipper* rocks over the wake of another vessel. How many other ships did the Frenchmen encounter in these waters? Had they sailed into a void? A thin line begins to rise on the horizon, then the roundish lump of the red brick Fort Massachusetts takes shape.

The island is under the protection and management of the National Park Service and a park ranger rides the boat out and prepares visitors for what they will find—an old Civil War era fort and a pristine, tropic-like beach of dazzling white sand.

Hurricane Camille, one of the worse storms ever experienced

Fort Massachusetts, pier and excursion boat, Ship Island.

in the USA, ripped a channel across Ship Island in 1969. Now the island, about nine miles long, is called East Ship and West Ship. West Ship is where the fort is located and is the destination of the *Pan American Clipper*. After allowing for Camille's channel, a visitor can imagine the island is much as it has been since it came into being about 3000 or 4000 years ago. The wind, sand and sea regularly sweep the island free of man-made structures. Fort Massachusetts (built 1859–1866) probably has the longest survival record.

According to legend the French built a fort here as well as a warehouse around 1717 and as early as 1724, the story goes, pine lumber was shipped via the island. The Mississippi Sound between Ship Island and the main land is only about 12 feet at its deepest. Small boats with shallow drafts would ferry cargo back and forth across the sound from the large ships in the deep water anchorage at *Isle aux Vaisseaux,* the French name for the island.

Probably among the first white women to visit the island were Frenchwomen "culled" from the prisons, hospitals (orphanages) or "houses of correction" of France and shipped out to the colonists as potential brides. The French government (through its agent John Law's Company of the Indies) provided several shipments of these young women with a small case containing a "marriage outfit," thus earning them the name of the *casettes* girls. Old records indicate the first contingents of unordered brides were not particularly well received. The early colonists preferred to marry native women, but the shipments of state-selected brides continued. Documents record the landing of the third group of *casettes* girls at Ship Island on January 5, 1721. Local historians claim this group of *casettes* girls were orphans, particularly virtuous and chaperoned by nuns.

The park rangers enthusiastically tell a story of the British landing 10,000 men on the island during the War of 1812. Records show that a British fleet of about 60 warships and auxiliary vessels anchored here on its way to the Battle of New Orleans in December 1814. This huge fleet carried not only soldiers, sailors and marines, but a civil government with all the prerequisite clerks ready to be installed when the British ousted the Americans in the prized port city. The wives, families and household goods of many of the men were also on the ships—they were not planning on a defeat. The strategic importance of Ship Island as a sentinel on the "short cut" run to New Orleans via Lakes Borgne and Ponchartrain became apparent as the invaders' armada sat smugly at anchorage in the harbor.

The War of 1812 inspired the U.S. War Department to begin planning and building a series of forts as a first line of defense along the coasts of the nation. Though Ship Island was declared a military reservation in 1847, Congress did not authorize the construction of a fort for nine years.

The Army Corps of Engineers began construction of the red brick and masonry fort in 1859. As the park rangers guide visitors through the twists and turns of the fortifications, they tell how difficult it was to entice civilian workers out to the island. They say laborers were paid $1.25 a day and charged 25 cents a day for room and board on the island. Carpenters, masons, blacksmiths and stonecutters made up the workforce that sometimes numbered 100 men. In 1861 when Mississippi seceded from the Union, the walls of the fort were only six to eight feet high.

Accounts of the next few months vary. Some legends claim that the beginning of the Civil War left the Federal garrison marooned and about May 1861 they destroyed the fort to keep the Confederates from seizing it. Other reports claim that an armed band of Mississippi Militia took possession of the un-finished fort as one of the first acts of the war within the state, but shortly thereafter abandoned it. Most accounts agree that by early July 1861, Confederate troops were back on the island with several mounted cannons. On July 9 the Confederates and the *USS Massachusetts* exchanged cannon fire for about 20 minutes without much damage to either side. This was the only direct military action the island saw during the war. For the rest of the summer the Confederates are said to have used sandbags and timbers to strengthen the walls of the unfinished fort only to abandon it and the island in September.

Union forces quickly filled the vacuum. From the island they staged their attack on New Orleans and in the spring of 1862 captured that city. The Union made good use of the island during the remainder of the war. They built over 40 wooden buildings (some Southern accounts say they denuded the western end of the island, turning it into a desert) and one of the US Army's first black regiments was recruited in Louisiana and stationed on the island. The island became a prisoner of war camp for captured Confederate military men as well as rebel/civilian political prisoners. But during the war years and afterwards, the island also had a goodly share of imprisoned Union soldiers. From 1862 to 1870 a Federal military prison stockade housed as many as 1000 military convicts.

As many as 4000 Confederate POWs were held on the island, as well as a notorious Mrs. Phillip Phillips of New Orleans. It seems Mrs. Phillips was in a good humor the day the funeral procession of a Union officer was passing her house and happened to laugh aloud. This offense coupled with the fact that she had previously been accused of teaching her children to spit on Union officers and had been particularly jubilant after a Union defeat in battle earned her Union General Benjamin "Beast" Butler's disgust. She was sentenced to the island. She was allowed to bring one female servant with her and was given a cell within the island hospital and a prisoner's ration of food and consideration.

Often Union soldiers as well as their prisoners succumbed to the rigors of the island. Over 230 Union troops were buried on the island but after the war their remains were removed to the Chalmette National Cemetery near New Orleans. An untold number of Confederate POWs were buried in the sand and for decades the shifting sands of the island, stirred by raging tropical storms, exposed their bones at will. Rather than a "Plymouth Rock" of the region as the island has been called by some historians, Ship Island could better be remembered as the region's Devil's Island.

In 1862 the Army Corps of Engineers recommended construction of the fort. During the war building materials often had to come from as far away as New England. And while the fort is surrounded with brick facades, its core between the brick walls is concrete. The brickwork at the fort is considered especially fine by experts. The careful lines and details of the walls and stairways are uncommon in surviving coastal fortifications. By the time the fort was completed and its allotment of guns installed (after the war in 1866), it was obsolete. One gargantuan 15-inch Rodman, the barrel of which weighs 50,000 pounds, still points towards the approaches to the pass leading to New Orleans. An ordnance-sergeant was in charge of the fort until 1903. At that time the Ship Island lighthouse keeper became the fort's caretaker. Several decades later a coastal branch of the American Legion bought the fort and used it as a site for various forms of merry-making. It did not come into the care of the National Park Service until 1971.

Other structures on the island have included lighthouses (the last one burned in 1972), and a quarantine station built on the east end of the island about 1880 in an attempt to combat yellow fever. In the 1890's the island was one of the busiest lumber ports in the United States, but with the building of the harbor at Gulfport, it had lost much of its commercial importance by 1900.

Park rangers slap at gnats and tell of old journal entries relating how the walls of the soldiers barrack were literally covered with mosquitoes at times during the Civil War. The insects aren't quite that bad now, but wary travelers come to the island equipped with repellant.

Fort Massachusetts, which by the way was never officially named—old maps have it marked as the Ship Island Fort—may have picked up the Massachusetts designation in its name from the engagement of the Confederate island battery with the Union warship. There is also a story that claims it was named for the home state of the Union General Benjamin "Beast" Butler who ruled New Orleans under martial law.

Visitors can become beachcombers on the glistening southern shore of the island. A fascination with the exotic offerings the sea leaves on the sand has long lured island sojourners to the water's edge. French colonists, British soldiers, lonely lighthouse keepers, American soldiers and generations of tourists have strolled the island's sands, listened to the surf, tasted the windborn saltspray in an ongoing chain of human visitations to this exotic spot that periodically wipes itself clean of all manifestations of the visits.

Ship Island is located about 12 miles south of Biloxi. From April through September excursion boats provide transportation to the island from Gulfport and Biloxi for a fee. The island is accessible year-round to private boats. Admission to the island and Fort Massachusetts is free.

A bath house with cold showers is open year-round. A snack bar is open daily during the summer months. Lifeguards are only on duty on the south beach during the summer. A ranger is on duty on the island throughout the year.

Ship Island and Fort Massachusetts are administered by the U.S. National Park Service as part of Gulf Island National Seashore. For more information write: Assistant Superintendent, 3500 Park Road, Ocean Springs, MS 39564. Telephone 601-875-9057.

Excursion boats to Ship Island leave from the pier behind the Buena Vista Motel, US 90, Biloxi and from the Gulfport Small Craft Harbor, US 90 near the intersection with US 49, Gulfport. Both excursion points are well marked with signs. Admission fee charged.

40

Some special places and times— Ripley Trade Day, Neshoba County Fair, and Salem Camp Meeting

Some Mississippi places of historic interest can best be appreciated on special occasions. Many towns and communities make private homes of unusual interest as well as unique private collections accessible to the public during their annual pilgrimages.

Carrollton, east of Greenwood on US 82, with 66 sites on the National Register of Historic Places, will warm the heart of any antebellum/Victorian architecture devotee during its spring pilgrimage rituals.

Lawrence County (the county seat is Monticello, about 60 miles west of Hattiesburg on US 84) features the rough-hewn "pioneer" architecture of the area and demonstrations of early crafts at its pilgrimages each April.

Other Mississippi places come alive at their own prescribed time but without the formality of a pilgrimage. For Ripley the time comes once a month on First Monday Trade Day. The first Trade Day, in the summer of 1893, drew such positive response that it has continued. Over the years it has moved from the courthouse square where the coroner-and-ranger conducted his estray sales, the sheriff made his necessary sales, the downtown merchants always marked down their merchandise and anyone with land, horses or stock "of any kind" sold their goods. Anybody with anything to sell is still invited, but the trade day has moved to an abandoned drive-in theatre on the edge of town.

Twenty-seven acres of economic chaos is one description of

this on-going folk happening. Spots are allotted for 600 traders, who pay a small fee and spread their wares on the ground, on the hood of their cars or set up booths. Some vendors come so frequently they have set up a semi-permanent western store-front-styled street that runs for about a block. The hours are roughly from daylight to dark. But this is no carefully organized event. Vendors sometimes open up for business as early as Thursday before First Monday. Sunday before First Monday is usually the biggest day of the gargantuan flea market. Wanna buy a chicken? Have your ears pierced? Some booths are portable department stores, others highly specialized shops. The latest electronic equipment, hand-embroidered Mexican blouses, produce, string beans, tomatoes, shoes and furniture line the rows made by the vendors. There are craftsmen work-ing on the spot, a rough-hewn pavilion where you can listen to amateur musicians and see ethnic food such as fried pork skins cooked as customers watch.

Ripley, at the intersection of MS 4 and MS 15, celebrates First Monday Trade Day every month. The trade grounds are at the edge of town on Highway 15. "If I had to describe it, I'd just call it entertainment," a Ripley resident said.

Entertainment might also be a fitting description of the Neshoba County Fair. Most of the year the fairgrounds, in a rural stretch of the red dirt county, are a ghost town, but for a couple of weeks each summer, the fairgrounds' buildings shed their dust covers and boarded windows to explode with a country fair's sounds and colors—high school bands and ca-rousels, red, white and blue banners draped over railings and pennants flying from the ferris wheels. Not only is the Neshoba County Fair entertaining, it is a fantasy, a dream world come true and it has been coming true around the last of July—first of August for just about 100 years.

There's a midway, with candied apples and cotton candy; there are painted ponies on the merry-go-rounds and real ones on the racetrack each afternoon; there are exhibits of canned goods, handmade quilts and quality livestock; and politicians venting excess rhetoric. The thing that's different about this fair is the whimsical, make-believe-world houses on the grounds.

Street scene from the Neshoba County Fair.

Harness racing, Neshoba County Fair.

The Neshoba County Fair is a live-in fair.

There are about 600 houses flaunting shades and hues—including pink, lavender, blue, yellow and red—that delight the eye with their disregard for uniformity. Some sit high off the ground, seemingly braced up by little more than imagination. These are grown-up children's playhouses—that require no locks, that are stocked with furniture scraping won't hurt, and dishes that chipping won't damage. Doors and windows stand open. Hospitality beckons. There is time at the fair—for visiting, befriending strangers, re-newing acquaintances, playing cards, rocking on the front porch and talking to children. The fair is a trip backward into half-remembered dreams of childhood, where life was a joyous event to be savored.

On the Mississippi frontier religion was also a joyous event to be savored. The Salem Camp meeting, lasting one week each October, near the Jackson-George counties' border, reminds visitors how Piney Woods pioneers crammed in as many sermons and services as possible at the then popular yearly religious happenings. Most frontier communities did not have a regular preacher or regular church services. They often saved their religious fervor for visits of a traveling evangelist or circuit riding preacher. With their harvests completed each fall, and a visiting preacher engaged for the occasion, many took a break from their chores and congregated for a marathon religious session.

Today sermons begin at 7:30 each morning and continue to be held during four well-spaced one-hour intervals throughout the day. Each service is announced by a visiting preacher blowing on a conch shell. In between services people visit, have family reunions, fill in gaps on their genealogical charts, eat and read the Bible.

Salem claims to be Mississippi's oldest active camp meeting. The first in 1826 was recorded for posterity in letters the settlers wrote to relatives in Georgia. The event has been cancelled only twice since 1826. There were no camp meetings in 1863 and 1864. One year's cancellation was due to the Civil War, the other to yellow fever.

Twenty-two families belong to the Salem Camp meeting

Association; they are descendants of the founding members and own the 22 cabins or "tents" surrounding the campground's square. In the special language of the camp meeting, those who spend the week in their cabins on the square are said to be "tenting." A 23rd cabin is called the "public tent." It's actually a concession stand specializing in carnival food (hot dogs and cotton candy) operated by the local Shriners. The rough-hewn tabernacle with its open sides is in the center of the square.

 Most "tents" consist of a wide central hallway, used for dining, with a room on either side for sleeping—one room for females, the other for males. Mattresses are placed on a built-in raised platform called a "Methodist pallet." In the back portion of the "tents," there is usually a kitchen, some of which are equipped with wood-burning stoves. Many of the dirt floors are still covered with pine straw, but slowly the camp meeting is succumbing to modern conveniences like indoor toilets and concrete floors. The oldest "tenters" say the biggest improvement at the camp meeting since their childhood has been electric lights and electric refrigerators. Before electricity came to Salem, after-dark activities were lighted by pinewood fires or torches and food spoiled easily.

Salem Camp Meeting, an early South Mississippi thanksgiving celebration, holds tight to tradition and though the association is officially Methodist, the services are so basically old southwest frontier that they represent a historic theological perspective that offers special insight into the character of the early Piney Woods pioneers.

For a calendar of special events throughout the state write: *Calendar,* Division of Tourism, P.O. Box 22825, Jackson, MS 39205. The calendar is published three times a year.

Carrollton Pilgrimage information is offered by the Carroll Society for the Preservation of Antiquities, Carrollton, Mississippi 38917. Admission fees charged for pilgrimage.

Lawrence County's Pilgrimage information is available from the Lawrence County Historical Society, P.O. Box 100, Monticello, MS 39654. Telephone 601-587-7175. Admission fee charged for pilgrimage.

Neshoba County Fair information is available from Courtney Tannehill, Box 207, Philadelphia, MS 39350. Telephone 601-656-4422. Fairgrounds are located on MS 21, about 14 miles southwest of Philadelphia. Admission fee charged to the fairgrounds.

Salem Camp Meeting Grounds are located in a remote area of Jackson County, near the George County line, about 14 miles south of Lucedale. The camp meeting is held annually in October. For more information, contact the Lucedale Chamber of Commerce, P.O. Box 912, Lucedale, MS 39452. Telephone 601-947-2880.

Ripley, at the intersection MS 4 and MS 15, celebrates First Monday Trade Day every month. The trade grounds are at the edge of town on Highway 15.

Index
of some major sites and attractions: